GERMANY

Modern and historical times: No other city in Germany can boast such an impressive skyline as banking metropolis Frankfurt am Main. Emperors were once crowned in the city's Gothic cathedral.

FASCINATING EARTH
GERMANY

The epitome of German Romanticism: High above the old city of Heidelberg stand the ruins of the Electoral castle; its most famous section, Ottoheinrichsbau, dates from the Renaissance period.

ABOUT THIS BOOK

Wherefore always seek still farther, when the good it lies so near?
Will you always seek still farther? See the good that lies so near.
Learn at once to grasp your fortune, Then happiness is always there.

Johann Wolfgang von Goethe, from his poem "Erinnerung" (Memory).

Germany, a land of contrasts, between oceans and mountains, rich in natural beauty and breathtaking landscapes: from the Wadden Sea flats on the North Sea coast and Rügen's chalk cliffs to the forested mountains at its heart and the romantic meandering courses of Rhine, Moselle, Neckar and Danube, down to the breathtaking limestone crags of the Alps in the south. And the country's cultural treasures are no less diverse and exquisite; teeming metropolises with world-famous architecture and museums, magnificent castles and monasteries, medieval towns and idyllic countryside settings concealing cultural jewels, centers of sporting or leisure activities.

This volume is a photographic voyage of discovery through Germany. The large-format full color illustrations offer new perspectives on the rich beauty on our doorstep. Our journeys take us through all Germany's states, exploring their enormous diversity, from Schleswig-Holstein in the north to the Bavarian Alps in the south. In addition to significant cultural areas, cities and locations, many protected as UNESCO World Cultural or Natural Heritage sites, this volume includes detailed features on historical, cultural and culinary topics to highlight additional aspects and offer valuable background information. The compact accompanying texts explain key historical or political contexts and direct attention to essential areas.

The picture section, subdivided geographically, is followed by an atlas section for rapid, easy location of the individual sights. The index at the end links the picture and atlas sections, and also includes important internet addresses for further orientation. Why seek farther? Follow Goethe's advice and join this magical journey through Germany's familiar and unknown ground, rediscovering and exploring anew.

The Publisher

Evening atmosphere on the pier at Sellin on the island of Rügen. 394 m long, the pier was reconstructed to original plans in the 1990s and is certainly the most beautiful on the Baltic coast.

CONTENTS

The port of Hamburg is one of the biggest in Europe. Its large fleet of tugs is a familiar sight, guiding mighty ships safely from the mouth of the Elbe to the quays and back. The landmark of the Eiderstedt peninsula is the Westerhever lighthouse, flanked by two identical houses. Not only is the lighthouse itself visible for miles; its signal light can be seen from up to 50 km away.

SCHLESWIG-HOLSTEIN, HAMBURG

Schleswig-Holstein – the "land between the seas," between the calm Baltic Sea and the often storm-tossed North Sea is a delightful tapestry of wooded alluvial hills and lakes. Mighty red-brick churches, thatched farmhouses and a host of museums bear witness to the rich cultural life of Germany's most northerly state. Around 100 km from the North Sea, on the Elbe, lies the Free Hanseatic City of Hamburg, a center of trade and a flourishing port that looks back on centuries of history.

Heligoland's landmark is the 48-m-high rock spur "Long Anna," now with structural concrete cladding to prevent it from collapse. Below, top to bottom: Heligoland's rocks are also home to countless seabirds, offering nesting places for guillemots, a characteristic feature of the island, gannets and razorbills. The northerly beach of the dunes is a refuge for common and gray seals (main picture), which can be viewed in closer proximity here than anywhere else in Germany.

HELIGOLAND

Geological and historical research shows that around the year 800, Heligoland was still part of a large island with 190 km of coastline. Today, the islet is no more than one sq km in area, and is composed of a conglomerate of red sandstone rocks towering 60 m out of the sea, and an adjacent area of dunes. Despite its size, the island has repeatedly been the object of invasion. Around 1400, the island, inhabited by Frisians, joined the Duchy of Schleswig-Holstein. Conquered by the British Navy in 1807, it was returned to Germany in 1890 in exchange for Zanzibar, and a naval base was established. After World War II, the British Air Force used the island for target practice, and it was not returned to Germany again until 1952. The people of Heligoland once lived from fishing, and the local lobster is still a prized delicacy. However, tourism has replaced fishing as the island's main source of income. Heligoland's tourist industry began when a seaside resort was built in 1826. At first, visitors were few, attracted by the island's fresh air and isolation. Today, Germany's only high-sea island is the destination for daily scheduled and excursion shipping. An ancient privilege gives Heligoland's fishermen the right to transport day visitors from ship to shore in their traditional "Börteboot" craft.

The main sight in the city of Schleswig is St Peter's Cathedral, built from 1134. Its interior (main picture) contains a masterpiece of European woodcarving, the Bordesholm Altar by Hans Brüggemann (1521). Not far from Schleswig and its archeological site, Haithabu Viking Museum (below) documents the culture of the Vikings. Glücksburg, with its moated castle of the same name, lies near the border between Schleswig and Denmark (top).

Schleswig

The name Schleswig means many things; a city, a historical duchy and bishopric, a landscape region, and the northern part of the state of Schleswig-Holstein. The city of Schleswig can look back on a rich and glorious history. Originally known as Haithabu, it was once an important hub of Viking trade. The new city of Schleswig, erected on the northern bank of the Schlei, became the center of the duchy of Schleswig in the Middle Ages, with Gottorf Castle as its magnificent residence. In the 19th century, the city was home to the Schleswig-Holstein nationalist movement. From 1868 to 1945, Schleswig was the capital of the Prussian province of Schleswig-Holstein. Today, the most important testimonials in stone to this lengthy history are the cathedral and Gottorf Castle, which today houses the collections of Schleswig-Holstein's regional museums.

Nature and man have impressed their unique signatures on the island of Sylt. Mighty dunes, reed-thatched houses, towering cliffs, the St Severin church in Keitum (below, from top), the lighthouse at Ostellenbogen (below and main picture), yacht ports, sleek cars and traditional wicker beach chairs (top, from left) – all these go to make up the island's austere romantic charm.

Sylt

The North Sea island of Sylt extends along the coast of Schleswig-Holstein like a giant breakwater. Although the first written records of Sylt date from the 13th century, its many mound graves indicate that it was inhabited in prehistoric times. For centuries, the island-dwellers lived as sailors, pirates and whalers, until they discovered tourism as a source of income. The new sea bathing resort of Westerland opened in 1857. Today, there are 12 villages on Germany's largest North Sea island, each with its own unique charm – from exclusive Kampen, a meeting-point for the rich and beautiful, to idyllic Keitum with reed-thatched brick houses. The island's unique and spellbinding natural scenery includes grand shifting sand-dunes that can be up to 1,000 m long and 35 m high, endless windswept sandy beaches and the crashing surf of the North Sea.

The Wadden Sea, drained daily by tides, is a unique biotope with a wide variety of fauna, including shore crabs, common seals and plaice (left, from top). But it is also a cultivated landscape; cattle graze on the Hallig islets (top). The main picture shows the cliffs at Morsum.

WADDEN SEA NATIONAL PARK

Nature conservation began along the German North Sea coast as early as 1909, with the foundation of the Jordsand Association. The Association bought the Hallig islet of Norderoog and declared it a nature reserve for sea-birds. Since then, awareness has grown that the Wadden Sea is a unique natural region that reacts sensitively to human intervention and can easily lose its ecological balance. 1985, 1986 and 1990 thus saw the foundation of the Wadden Sea National Park, extending over the three states of Schleswig-Holstein, Hamburg and Lower Saxony. The constant ebb and flow of the tides has created a landscape of coastal wetlands that is constantly changing. The Wadden Sea National Park is home to more than 10 million birds every year; while most are migratory, many also breed here. The common seal population is estimated at 16,000, together with a colony of gray seals. Several thousand porpoises live in the sea around North Frisia. In a cultivated landscape such as the Wadden Sea, the altruistic goal is to leave nature to its own devices. The fishing industry leaves its mark, while more serious problems are caused by pollutants from rivers and the use of fertilizers. Continued wide-ranging efforts will be needed if the unique Wadden Sea landscape is to be preserved.

In Schleswig-Holstein, water is a dominant element, not only on the coast but also inland: on Plöner See with Plön Castle in the Holsteinische Schweiz region (top), at Eutin, on Ratzeburg Lake in the Lauenburgisches Land region, or Schaalsee. Towns such as Ratzeburg also offer Romanesque brick churches and impressive market squares (below, from top). The tranquil port of Ort on the island of Fehmarn is an invitation to wander (main picture).

Fehmarn, Holsteinische Schweiz, Lauenburg Lakes

The glaciers of the Ice Age and frequent fluctuations in sea level have shaped the landscape of Schleswig-Holstein's Baltic coast and hinterland. The region known as Holsteinische Schweiz (Holstein's Switzerland) between Kiel and Lübeck Bays, is a gently rolling expanse of hills clothed with beech forests. Eutin, the "Weimar of the North," is the largest town in the region, receiving its name from the first holidaymakers to come here in the 19th century. On the deep Baltic bays or fjords lie cities such as Kiel, already an important center in the era of the Hanseatic League. Today, sailing, fishing and agriculture, with tourism in the coastal resorts, are the main sources of income in Holstein. Fehmarn, Germany's second largest island, lies off the coast of East Holstein and is an important point on the shortest ferry route to Scandinavia, the "Vogelfluglinie" (bird flight line).

Many of Lübeck's buildings bear witness to the power and wealth of past eras. The most famous is probably Holstentor gate, flanked by the two churches of St Mary and St Peter (main picture). The Heiligen-Geist-Hospital has an impressive exterior, as do the Holstentor and City Hall (top, from left). Pictures opposite: Interior of Heilig-Geist-Hospital; historic "Schiffergesellschaft" restaurant; Holstenhafen port.

CONCORDIA DOMI FORIS PAX

Hanseatic City of Lübeck

Germany's largest Baltic port has a medieval center that still displays its past as a rich Hanseatic trading center. Count Adolf II of Holstein founded a merchants' colony in 1143 and named it after the Slav settlement Liubice; in 1226 the town was declared a Free Imperial City and rapidly advanced to become a key trading center. In 1358, Lübeck became the center of the Hanseatic League, but declined with the Reformation and the dissolution of the League in 1630. The Napoleonic Wars and later World War II wreaked considerable destruction. Lack of funds prevented Lübeck's historic center from being remodeled by replacing its ancient buildings with modern architecture, thus enabling the richly traditional trading metropolis to preserve its vibrant medieval atmosphere and flair, with its old quarter surrounded by water.

Hamburg's appearance has always been shaped by water. Magnificent views over the Binnenalster lake to the Jungfernstieg promenade (below, from top), the City Hall (also main picture) and Aussenalster lake with an almost nautical feel. Plenty of fun is available at the "Dom" funfair on Heiligengeistfeld, and of course at the famous St Pauli district, with the Reeperbahn and famous Davidswache police station (top).

Hanseatic City of Hamburg

Hamburg, once a major Hanseatic city, looks back on a glorious past. Even today, the city is Germany's largest and most important port and a metropolis with a rich array of culture and many gardens and parks. Water is ubiquitous in this Free Hanseatic City: the port extending along both sides of the River Elbe, the many drainage channels or "Fleete" that run through the city, and the Binnenalster lake in the city's center with its elegant and prestigious promenades such as the Jungfernstieg. Almost all the city is criss-crossed by a network of waterways, which include the Elbe, the Außenalster and a maze of navigable canals. Elegant villas and parks, including the famous Planten un Blomen park, fringe the banks, as in the exclusive district of Blankenese, bearing witness to the past wealth and commercial and social status of the Hanseatic merchants.

Always a fascinating sight: the big ships in the Port of Hamburg's dry docks (main picture) and the passing tugs, cutters and freighters. In the Speicherstadt ("warehouse") district, tea and coffee are still stored today (top). The Fischmarkt (below) is a lively and often raucous market.

Germany | Schleswig-Holstein, Hamburg

PORT OF HAMBURG

Germany's largest port is still the economic heart of the Free and Hanseatic City of Hamburg, as even landlubbers will spot when touring the port. The history of the Port of Hamburg began in the 12th century, when Count Adolf III of Holstein built his new city and port next to the existing episcopal city. Hamburg soon rose to become a leading power in the Hanseatic League, and as early as the 14th century was the most important reloading point between the North and Baltic Seas. When overseas trading began, Hamburg became Germany's gateway to the world. 1880 saw a milestone in this story with the construction of the Free Port and the world's largest complex of warehouses, the "Speicherstadt," built in Gothic-inspired style in North German brick. Around this period, the shipyard of Blohm & Voss was founded, with its mighty dry docks forming an arresting sight from the St Pauli landing-stages. Today, over 10,000 ships from around 100 countries are loaded and unloaded in the port every year. Container shipping is playing an important role, and Hamburg's port has one of the world's most modern container terminals, handling more than six million containers in 2003 alone. Major extension to the port's infrastructure is planned for the upcoming decades, in line with forecast increases in cargo volume.

Windmills are the emblem of East Frisia. Many are now used as museums or holiday homes, like this Dutch-style windmill from 1802 on the River Harle at Altfunnixsiel (below). 1889 saw the foundation of the artists' colony at Worpswede. Artists including Heinrich Vogeler settled in this village near Bremen and established a colony that is still a center of art today. Main picture: the "Haus im Schluh".

LOWER SAXONY, BREMEN

The countryside in Lower Saxony is richly varied, from the Wadden mudflats to the Harz Mountains. And the region's economic structure is as diverse as its landscapes; in addition to agriculture, the raw materials industry is of prime significance (petroleum, natural gas, coal, salt, mineral ores). Wolfsburg is the center of the automotive industry, and Hanover hosts major trade shows such as Cebit. The city-state of Bremen has a maritime flair; Bremen city is shaped by trade, while its "offshoot" Bremerhaven, is a major port.

Like a string of pearls, the East Frisian islands of Borkum, Juist, Norderney, Baltrum, Langeroog, Spiekeroog and Wangerooge extend along the North Sea coastline between Emden and Wilhelmshaven. The prevailing natural features of these islets, which often consist of a single hamlet, are their dunes tufted with marram grass, such as here in Juist (main picture). One of the best-known coastal resorts is Greetsiel, with its port crowded with bright fishing boats and its twin windmills (top). Windmills can also be seen farther inland in East Frisia's flat fen landscape, crisscrossed by canals and ditches. Opposite: the windmill at Sande-Neustadtgödens.

East Frisia

The sea and its tidal forces have ruled life in the broad coastal regions between the Rivers Weser and Ems since primeval times. The area has been the birthplace of many a seafarer and whaler, who contributed to the growth of trading cities such as Emden. Inland, the broad plains of East Frisia unfurl with their wide moors and meadows. East Frisia is also a paradise for enthusiasts of old windmills, which rise clearly visible for many miles above the flat land. The East Frisians were quick to harness the power of the wind for land drainage and flour and oil production. Today, extensive wind parks supply power in East Frisia. The die-straight fen channels, originally used by the colonists to make the moor areas cultivable, also offer a fascinating view. Papenburg alone, the oldest fen colony, is criss-crossed by channels totalling 40 km in length.

Bremen's pride and joy is the market square, with the Gothic cathedral of St Peter, the magnificent City Hall and "Stone Roland" statue (below). The city's port is still a significant economic force. The futuristic Universal Science Center has been a major visitor attraction since 2000 (top).

Hanseatic City of Bremen

Despite widespread destruction in the World War II, Bremen, which together with Bremerhaven forms Germany's smallest state, still boasts many historic works of architecture in both original and restored conditions. The city on the River Weser developed from a fishing and trading settlement and experienced its first cultural and economic heyday in the 11th century. In 1358, Bremen joined the Hanseatic League and became a Free Imperial City in 1646. Bremen's most attractive district is the historic city center around the market square, with its chief glory the 15th-century City Hall. Directly in front of it is a further significant monument, the imposing statue of Roland from 1404. Bremerhaven to the north of Bremen, was founded in 1827 as the city's outer port. Today, it is famous as a fishing, shipping and polar research center.

In the sandy soil of Lüneburg Heath, ling, juniper and birch trees thrive. This unique cultivated landscape provides grazing for a special breed of moorland sheep known as "Heidschnucken". The region is still marked by extensive agriculture, scattered with old towns of half-timbered buildings such as Celle (large picture opposite). The Altes Land (Old Country) region, with its impressive brick and half-timbered farmhouses, is particularly beautiful in spring when the orchards bloom. Stade's glorious past is recalled today by its old quarter and historic Hanseatic port (top, from left). The opposite pictures (bottom) show the Gerichtslaube (Court Arbor) in Lüneburg's courthouse and the church of St Martin in Uelzen.

Altes Land, Stade Geest, Lüneburg Heath

The Altes Land region lies at the gates of Hamburg. In the spring, up to eight million fruit trees transform the country, scattered with farm villages in traditional horseshoe layout, into a sea of blossom. Its old estates and impressive farmhouses are also worth seeing. The towns and villages in the bordering plains region of Stade Geest are tranquil places; Apensen with early stone graves, Horneburg with its legend of Isern Hinnerk (Iron Henry), or Himmelpforten with its attractive town museum. Deserted countryside, sand tracks, birch copses, heather, wild sheep, watermills – Lüneburg Heath is all this and more. But its fascination today derives from centuries of depletion and exhaustive cultivation. As late as the Middle Ages, the region was covered with dense forests of oak, pine and birch. They were felled as fuel for the salt works, leaving the expanse of moorland we know today.

A striking feature of Braunschweig's Burgplatz square, fringed by St Blasius Cathedral and Dankwarderode Castle, is the proud Castle Lion statue, the city's heraldic animal (main picture and below). The magnificent Romanesque Church of St Michael in Hildesheim has superb paintings on the wooden ceiling portraying the Tree of Jesse, the family tree of Christ. Created around 1230, this work is composed of 1300 individual sections and is a unique example of Romanesque monumental art. By contrast, Trinity Church (top) on Wolfenbüttel's Holzmarkt has ornate baroque lines.

Braunschweig, Hildesheim, Wolfenbüttel

The Braunschweig region offers an array of important historical works of art. Henry the Lion selected the "Bruneswiek" area to build Dankwartsrode Castle, and awarded the site the status of a city. In 1753 the city became the imperial residence of the Dukes of Braunschweig, who had formerly resided in Wolfenbüttel. Under these rulers, Wolfenbüttel, with its richly half-timbered architecture, was a center of the arts and sciences and became famous as the site of the Library of Duke August, founded in 1572 and once Europe's largest library. The collection of 12,000 ancient manuscripts includes the Lectionary of Henry the Lion. Although Hildesheim was largely destroyed in 1945, many historic buildings have since been restored, such as the Market Square with Knochenhaueramtshaus (Butchers' Guild Hall), the Romanesque cathedral and the Church of St Michael.

Welfenschloss castle in Herzberg was constructed entirely in half-timbering (main picture). In Goslar, murals (of Barbarossa and Henry the Lion), the Kaiserhaus and the grave of Henry III (top, from left) hark back to the former Imperial Palace. Bizarre rock formations, such as Rabenklippen or Kästeklippen, are found in the Hochharz region (opposite).

Harz Foothills, Oberharz, Hochharz

The Harz, a region steeped in myths and legends, is Germany's northernmost mountain range. The part in the state of Lower Saxony, Oberharz, was already a major economic center in the Middle Ages. Oberharz, with its wooded mountains and craggy valleys, is popular with hikers and winter sports enthusiasts alike. Its highest peak is Wurmberg at 971 m. Over a millennium ago, Oberharz was already home to intensive forestry, water-power systems and metal ore mining – an ancient tradition amply demonstrated in the old silver center of Goslar, in the host of mining museums and the Mining Faculty at Clausthal-Zellerfeld. However, the agricultural countryside of the Harz foothills is little-known. Salzgitter and Wolfsburg are the dominant economic centers; the country between Göttingen and Hanover is marked by gentle rolling mountain ranges such as the Elm, Ith and Hils.

The breadth of styles in the Weser Renaissance is illustrated by the castles of Hämelschenburg and Bückeburg and the moated castle of Hülsede (top, from left). The magnificently ornamented castle chapel (main picture) and Golden Hall (bottom left) can be seen in Bückeburg castle.

WESER RENAISSANCE

The 100 years from 1520 saw the development of a unique architectural style in the catchment area of the River Weser, today forming the border between Lower Saxony and North Rhine-Westphalia. The "Weser Renaissance", as the period was known, was created by architects such as Jörg Unkair who absorbed inspiration from the Netherlands, France, Italy and Bohemia to create their own unique and diverse language of forms. This spate of building was made possible by a period of economic prosperity in the Weserbergland region, which at the time was the flourishing "bread basket of Germany." The nobility and landed gentry commissioned a host of new castles to be built in this style or had existing buildings redesigned. Between Hannoversch-Münden and Bremen, Bielefeld and Paderborn and in Alfeld, Wolfsburg and Celle lie castles such as Bevern, Hämelschenburg, Bückeberg, the Welfenschloss (Guelph Castle) in Gifhorn or Brake Castle at Lemgo, today home of the Weser Renaissance Museum. The region's cities were also enriched by council halls and half-timbered buildings in the Weser Renaissance style. Typical features of the architecture are richly ornamented facades, windowed gables, dormers, battlements and oriels, such as the magnificent examples in Höxter, Hamelin, Minden, Lemgo and Rinteln.

The Hanseatic city of Rostock on the River Warnow is steeped in history. Why not take a fascinating tour of the port with its old warehouses and Church of St Peter (below)? One of the most idyllic stretches of Baltic coastline in the Mecklenburg-Vorpommern region can be found at Ahrenshoop on the Fischland peninsula, where reed-thatched cottages huddle between the steep cliffs and the beach.

MECKLENBURG-VORPOMMERN

Endless sandy beaches, craggy cliffs, sand spits, bays, the coastal inlets known as "Bodden", woods extending into the hinterland, countless moorlands and lakes – in Mecklenburg-Vorpommern, vast stretches of the landscape are refreshingly unspoilt despite the region's increasingly intensive agriculture. It is home to well over half of Germany's population of cranes, eagles, otters and beavers. And between the lakes and hills lie castles and villages where time seems to have stood still.

Schwerin Castle took its present shape in the 19th century, when four buildings ranging from the 15th to 17th centuries were combined into one (main picture and opposite). Top, from left: view of Wismar's Old Market with the striking "Wasserkunst" (water art) pavilion, built around 1600. Nearby, one tower remains of St Mary's Church, destroyed in World War II.

Schwerin, Wismar

Schwerin, the old residence of the Dukes of Mecklenburg-Vorpommern, has been the capital of the state of Mecklenburg-Vorpommern since 1990. The city lies 100 km east of Hamburg amidst idyllic lakes. Its most important building is the castle, located on an island, with many turrets and oriels giving it a fairy-tale air. Other major works of architecture are the State Theater, the State Museum and the neoclassical Marstall (stables). The ancient Hanseatic city of Wismar, picturesquely located at the mouth of Wismar Bay between Lübeck and Rostock, has a beautiful old center with many gabled houses in Renaissance, baroque and brick Gothic style – including the "Alter Schwede" (Old Swede), the city's oldest burgher's house and a reminder that the city was in Swedish hands in the 17th and 18th centuries – and an Italianate court.

From the port, Rostock's skyline is dominated by St Mary's Church and the "Wohnhochhaus" apartment block on Lange Strasse, a rare blend of North German brick Gothic and Stalinist influences (main picture). The Old Market in Stralsund features St Nicholas' Church and the city hall with its decorative wall, one of the most attractive secular buildings in the brick Gothic style (below and top).

Rostock, Stralsund

Rich in tradition, the Hanseatic city of Rostock has never been the official capital of Mecklenburg, yet was always its most important city. Rostock University is the oldest in northern Europe; the international port is the region's gateway to the world and, with its wharves and factories, a driving force of the city's economy. The beautiful old quarter centers around the spacious New Market, with mighty St Mary's Church. Stralsund, also a Hanseatic city, has much valuable old architecture, with streets of brick Gothic buildings and merchants' houses dating from the 15th to the 19th centuries. The heart of the old city, enclosed by picturesque lakes and parks, is the Old Market, with the architectural jewels of the City Hall, crowned by magnificent gables, and Church of St Nicholas. Also well worth seeing are the churches of St Mary and St Jacob.

The richly varied landscape is characteristic of this stretch of the Baltic coast. To the north of Hiddensee Island rise the hills of Dornbusch, topped with a lighthouse (main picture). Top, from left: The coast of the Zingst peninsula, with craggy lime-stone cliffs and long, flat beaches. On the island of Rügen, in the Schmale Heide region between Proper Wiek and Jasmunder Bodden, the landscape is expansive and spacious. Bottom: Old sailing boats in the tranquil port of Ahrenshoop.

Vorpommersche Boddenlandschaft, Hiddensee Island

Germany's most northeasterly state has more expanses of unspoilt countryside than anywhere else in the country. Almost one-third of its area is covered by nature parks and reserves, the largest of which is Vorpommersche Boddenlandschaft, a natural saltwater and wetland paradise and home to many rare species of birds, amphibians and fish. An ecological jewel is the 6,000 ha of virgin forest on the Darß peninsula. Darß and the other peninsulas of Fischland and Zingst are popular recreational areas. Well-marked paths along picturesque craggy coastlines are inviting routes for long walks. Further east, the island of Hiddensee, still attached to Rügen before the great floods of 1308, offers richly diverse unspoilt landscapes. Cars are prohibited on the island, almost all of which is a conservation area. It is justifiably known as "dat soete Laenneken" (the sweet little land).

The cliffs of Jasmund National Park (main picture and below right) are Rügen's most spectacular landscape. This page, clockwise: Baabe's sandy beach; port at Gager; chalk cliffs of Stubbenkammer and Wissower Klinken (also top right).

Rügen

Where the Baltic gnaws tirelessly away at the chalk: Germany's largest island is only 50 km in diameter, but has several hundred km of coastline and breathtaking natural diversity. Rolling meadows and boggy moorlands rub shoulders with beech forests and two inland lakes, the Small and Large Jasmunder Boddens. While the southwest is predominantly flat and agricultural, other areas have steep crags falling to the sea. The famous painting by Caspar David Friedrich, the spearhead of the German Romantic movement who was born in 1774 in nearby Greifswald, made the "Chalk Cliffs on Rügen" world-famous. It showed the "Victoria Outlook" near the Wissower Klinken, now reduced to two stumps after crumbling spectacularly into the sea in 2005. The island is connected to the German mainland by a road and rail bridge.

Each individual health spa along the coast between Wismar and Swinemünde (Swinoujście) offers all the amenities of a full-scale exclusive resort, with beach promenades, piers and luxury hotels. The most glamorous surroundings are in Heiligendamm (main picture and below left, bottom picture), but Binz also has historical flair (top and below left, top two pictures).

THE KAISER'S RESORTS

It is not only the natural landscape of the Baltic coast that is impressive. The region's manmade creations are equally breathtaking – particularly when physical and mental well-being are involved. With its unique climate, its lakes and beaches and its wide range of health facilities, Mecklenburg-Vorpommern has an amazing 53 officially registered health resorts and spas, of which the most famous are the "imperial three" resorts of Bansin, Heringsdorf and Ahlbeck. Situated at the eastern end of the island of Usedom, near the Polish border, they exude a cosmopolitan style with their broad white beaches and luxury hotels. Binz, the Isle of Rügen's largest and most prestigious resort, is no less fashionable. The town is the starting-point for cruises to neighboring Baltic resorts and the "Chalk Cliffs". Its white villas with elaborately carved wood oriels, verandas and balconies create an air of filigree elegance. However, the title of Germany's oldest resort goes to Heiligendamm, known as the "white city by the sea" for its gleaming neoclassical houses. The town is in the municipality of Bad Doberan, once the summer residence of the Mecklenburg court. Today, Heiligendamm is one of Germany's most luxurious seaside resorts, building on decades of tradition as a retreat for Europe's aristocrats, and even for its royalty.

The emblems of Usedom's "imperial three" resorts are their impressive piers. Measuring 508 m in length, the pier at Heringsdorf (main picture) is the longest such structure in continental Europe. The pier in Ahlbeck (top) celebrated its 100th anniversary in 1990. In the hinterland and backwater, the peninsula of Gnitz, Karnin, Zempin and the Usedomer Winkel region offer unforgettable impressions (opposite, from top).

Usedom

The island of Usedom, almost 450 km in area, extends from the Peene to the Swina, two mouths of the River Oder. It is a paradise for holidaymakers, with bracing sea air and long expanses of beaches ideal for families; in fact, generations ago, this feature brought the island the nickname of "Berlin's bathtub." The old fishing settlements with reed-thatched houses are mainly clustered along the backwater, but toward the end of the 19th century, a row of elegant resorts were founded facing the open sea. The best-known of these are Bansin, Ahlbeck and Heringsdorf, known collectively as "the Nice of the North," which are linked by a boardwalk, but Koserow and Zinnowitz are also popular. Peenemünde, the former missile testing site on the western point of the island, was turned into an open-air museum of science history after the reunification of East and West Germany.

Water as far as the eye can see on Müritz lake at Röbel (main picture) and Waren (top right). The Mecklenburg lake region is not only home to nesting storks. Here, treasures of art and architecture can be found, such as the monastery church at Malchow, the castles at Basedow and Güstrow, or Neustrelitz castle park with Luisentempel and orangery (bottom, from left).

Mecklenburg's Lakes

The region between Schwerin and Uckermark, known as the Mecklenburg Lakes, has around a thousand lakes interlinked by rivers, channels and canals. The region was already popular with sports and recreation seekers during the German Democratic Republic. Canoe or boat tours of several days can be undertaken, past tranquil villages and delightful unspoilt landscapes. The largest lake is the Müritz, the catchment area of which became a 300 sq m national park in 1990. This paradise of virgin forest, bogland, meadows and reed-fringed lakes is a protected habitat for storks, cormorants, kingfishers, herons and eagles. The charming countryside between Malchin and Teterow, Malchin and Kummerower lakes is known as Mecklenburgische Schweiz (Mecklenburg's Switzerland) for its gently rolling hills and uplands, some reaching almost 200 m in height.

Charlottenburg, Berlin's largest and most beautiful castle, is in the Italianate baroque style. It was built toward the end of the 17th century for the Electress, later Queen, Sophie Charlotte. The magnificent parklands in Potsdam include the New Gardens where Frederick William II built the early classical Marble Palace at Heiliger See lake. To the left is the kitchen, designed as a classical temple.

BRANDENBURG, BERLIN

Berlin is Berlin. The past and present capital of Germany has developed at breathtaking pace. The seat of the country's parliament and government is also its political nerve center and, with its museums, theaters and architectural masterpieces, is once again the cultural metropolis of Germany. The region around Berlin is crowded with idyllic lakes, magnificent gardens and aristocrats' estates. In addition, Brandenburg offers stretches of largely unspoilt countryside, tranquil fishing villages and Hanseatic cities rich in tradition.

The baroque castle of Rheinsberg was built from 1736 to 1740 (main picture). Cistercian monasteries such as Zinna (below left) or Chorin (right) are among the most impressive testimonies to the brick Gothic style. The monastery of St Paul (center) in Brandenburg is from the same era. The statue in Neuruppin commemorates the birth of the great novelist Theodor Fontane there in 1819. This avenue of birch trees (top) dates from this time.

Schorfheide, Havelland, Fläming

The little town of Rheinsberg lies in the Mark of Brandenburg, almost 100 km to the north of Berlin in the region of Neuruppin. Like so many towns in this area that are steeped in history, Rheinsberg can trace its origins back to the Middle Ages, but its present-day classical face dates from a fire in the mid-18th century. Rheinsberg primarily owes its popularity to its castle of the same name, where the later Emperor Frederick II loved to stay when he was Crown Prince and which later became the home of his brother Henry. Designed by Georg Wenzeslaus von Knobelsdorff in graceful classical style, the castle on the banks of Grienerickesee received a literary commemoration in 1912 with the publication of Kurt Tucholsky's novel "Rheinsberg – A Picture-Book for Lovers". The castle now contains a memorial to the writer, known for his barbed pen.

The western end of the magnificent boulevard Unter den Linden is marked by the Brandenburg Gate, a focal point of Germany's turbulent history for more than 200 years and all too long a symbol of the country's divided capital (top). Farther east, "Old Fritz" high on his horse, once again presides over the historic heart of the multimillion-strong metropolis (below). The French Cathedral and Schauspielhaus theater are the focal points of Gendarmenmarkt square (main picture).

"Old" Berlin

200 years ago, Germany's old and new capital on the River Spree was already a playground for the finest architects. Their eye for classical proportions gave Berlin what is probably its most beautiful square – the Gendarmenmarkt. Named after the Gens d'Armes, the regiment of the soldier king Frederick William II, this spacious quadrangle was set out around 300 years ago as the marketplace of the new residential quarter, Friedrichstadt.

Huguenots, fleeing persecution in their rabidly Catholic homeland and welcomed by the Hohenzollerns with open arms, settled it. They built themselves a unique house of worship, with a magnificent exterior yet an interior of Protestant simplicity – the French Cathedral. The Schauspielhaus theater is a characteristically "antique" creation by Karl Friedrich Schinkel. At its reopening in 1984 it was officially renamed Konzerthaus (Concert Hall).

Symbolizing a new transparency in politics, the glass dome on the Reichstag (parliament building) attracts crowds of fascinated visitors to watch politicans in action, on the site where the Constitution was suspended in 1933 and the first pan-German parliament of the post-war period convened in 1990. The ruined Kaiser-Wilhelm-Gedächtniskirche (Memorial Church) on the Ku'damm, with its new extension (below) by Egon Eiermann, is a reminder of the era when democracy failed. Top: in the foreground the Philharmonie on Potsdamer Platz.

"New" Berlin

The glass dome designed by Sir Norman Foster that has crowned the old Reichstag since 1999 has become Berlin's new emblem. Not far away on Potsdamer Platz, a whole new city district arose after the fall of the Berlin Wall. Today, on what was once a yawning wasteland in the very heart of the city, a symphony of stone, steel and glass reaches toward the sky. The most impressive architecture in this drawing-board metropolis was created by two well-heeled developers: the glass Sony Center, designed by Helmut Jahn, is a plaza under a floating pavilion roof and includes a movie museum; Renzo Piano's Daimler-Chrysler Building has a less exalted purpose as an extensive shopping complex. Next to the casino and opposite the Philharmonie hall, built by Hans Scharoun from 1960 to 1963, the Musical Theater is the location of the star-studded annual Film Festival.

The scope of Berlin's museums is enormous, ranging from the East Side Gallery (below) on the east side of the Wall, to Daniel Libeskind's Jewish Museum. Other highlights include the bust of Nefertiti in the Egyptian Museum, the Gedächtniskirche, Mies van der Rohe's New National Gallery, the "Molecule Men," the Hamburger Bahnhof, showing contemporary art in a former station, and the sculpture exhibition in Friedrichwerdersche Kirche. Main picture: the Altes Museum, shown in festively illuminated glory. Top: bronze sculpture at the Altes Museum.

BERLIN: METROPOLIS OF THE ARTS

Berlin is home to around 170 museums and memorials, from the Bauhaus Archive or Bert Brecht's stamping-ground to the Vitra Design Museum. But the focus is on four museum groups, each with unique collections: The Dahlem museum complex, specialising in non-European art and culture; the museums in and around Charlot- tenburg castle, including the Berggruen Collection and the Brohän Museum; the Kulturforum to the west of Potsdamer Platz, including the Gemäldegalerie (Portrait Gallery) and the Neue Nationalgalerie (New National Gallery); the Museum of Musical Instruments and the Kunstgewerbemuseum (Museum of Applied Arts) and finally the historic nucleus of all the collections, the Museum Island, a UNESCO World Heritage Site. It comprises the Pergamon Museum with its collections of antique statuary and Vorderasiatisches (Middle Eastern) Museum, the Bode Museum with collections of painting and sculpture from medieval and Renaissance times, the Alte Nationalgalerie and the Altes Museum. The latter was designed by Schinkel and, with its elegant colonnaded front, is one of the world's most beautiful classical buildings. It houses part of the antique statuary collection. The most important memorials are the Holocaust Memorial and the memorial at the former Gestapo and SS headquarters.

Potsdam's historic districts include Alter Markt, where today Nikolaikirche church and the Altes Rathaus (Old City Hall) stand (top). Emperor William I built Babelsberg Castle (opposite) as a neo-Gothic residence. The ornamental wooden cabin is part of the Alexandrowka, a settlement for Russian allies of the Prussian Army in the Wars of Liberation. The main picture shows the Sacrow Heilandskirche church, consecrated in 1845.

Potsdam

The former residential city of the Hohenzollerns on the western edge of Berlin portrays the lighter side of the Prussian rulers – at least with regard to the fine arts. The old quarter alone can boast several testimonials to the Hohenzollerns' former glory. The main attractions are naturally Potsdam's castles, flanking the River Havel in extensive parklands. Another major attraction is the Heilandskirche church at Sacrow, reflected picturesquely in the river's surface, as designed by the paramount landscape gardener of the time, Peter Josef Lenné. At the time when Germany was divided into East and West the building achieved world fame when the Wall was sited to run directly along its edge. The last service was held here at Christmas 1961. Not until 28 years had passed and the no man's land of the Wall had been removed did the church resume its original function.

After the Seven Years' War, from 1763, King Frederick II commissioned the three-winged New Palace, shown here with actors and fireworks at the spectacular annual "Schlössernacht" celebrations. Top: the Roman Baths, designed by Schinkel, Sanssouci rising above terraced vineyards, and the Orangery in neo-Renaissance style.

Sanssouci

Sanssouci (without a care) described the way Frederick the Great wanted to spend his time at his Potsdam summer residence. He commissioned Georg Wenzeslaus von Knobelsdorff to build the graceful single-story summer retreat from 1745–1747, partly to Frederick's own designs and sited amidst terraces of vines. Richly ornamented with decorative statuary and stucco, it is a major work of German rococo and Potsdam's primary tourist attraction. The palace also bears witness to its inhabitant's musical interests; the king played flute in the music room, and in the magnificent library he held discussions with the great Enlightenment philosopher Voltaire. Further buildings were added, such as the Neue Kammern (New Chambers), the New Palace and, under Frederick's successors, the Orangery and Charlottenhof Castle. Peter Josef Lenné designed the grounds.

At the southern border of the Upper Spree Forest is Lehde open-air museum. The traditional way of life of the Sorbian farmers is documented in these Old Wendish farmyards, with several herb gardens and boat-builder's, blue-printing and potter's workshops.

Spreewald Forest

Berliners' favourite destination for excursions is less than an hour's drive to the southeast toward Cottbus, and is famous for more than its culinary speciality of pickled cucumbers. Spreewald is criss-crossed by a 1,000-km-long network of around 300 waterways known as "Fliessen". In 1991, UNESCO declared the area a biosphere reserve to protect the habitat of around 18,000 plant and animal species. 600 professional ferry operators ply their trade here within Europe's largest alder forests, carrying recreation-seeking city-dwellers into this unspoilt landscape in their traditional punt-like wooden boats propelled by poles. Only around half of the lowland area, which extends for a total of, 75 km long and up to 16 km wide, is used for agriculture by the native Sorb people – naturally by sustainable methods approved by ecologists.

The three sculptured building complexes of the Neuer Zollhof in Düsseldorf, designed by Frank O. Gehry, form a striking postmodern ensemble (below). Haus Bodelschwingh in Dortmund (main picture), a moated castle on a foundation of oak piers dating back to 1302, bears witness to the many different eras of architecture it has experienced through the ages, with elements of Gothic, Renaissance and Baroque.

NORTH RHINE WESTPHALIA

The most highly populated of all Germany's states, this region is noted for its wide range of landscapes. Routes through Münsterland and Teutoburger Wald run past lush meadows, romantic windmills and looming moated castles. But northern Rhineland is completely different from Westphalia, with teeming urban centers in Cologne and Düsseldorf. The Ruhr area, once synonymous with the coal and steel industries, has long undergone a structural sea-change and has many areas of natural beauty to offer.

In Warendorf near the Hengstparade, riders and teams go through their paces (right). In Münster, the arcades and gabled houses at the Prinzipalmarkt and St. Lamberti Church (main picture) are rich in historic flair – the same applies for the Erbdrostenhof's baroque hall (below).

Münsterland

Fortresses and moated castles, picturesque half-timbered villages and proud churches create the Münsterland region's unique atmosphere. The area between the Teutoburger Wald and the German-Dutch border is flat or gently rolling, with occasional higher hills. Small copses and hedges are characteristic of the landscape, and, dotted with a host of castles, create an almost park-like atmosphere. Agriculture and horse-breeding are prac-

tised and have left their mark on the countryside. The center of the region is the venerable university city of Münster, which gave the area its name. Its well-preserved historic old quarter has many treasures, including the Romano-Gothic cathedral of St Paul, the magnificent Lambertikirche, dating from the 14th to the 15th century, the baroque Stadtschloss castle, and the attractive arcades and tiered gable-roofed houses.

In addition to Schloss Nordkirchen (main picture), interesting sights are the moated castles of Raesfeld, Wasterwinkel, Lembeck, Vischering, Anholt and Gemen (below right, clockwise). Top, from left: gardens of Schloss Nordkirchen; Anholt Castle with baroque statuary.

MOATED CASTLES

Probably no other region of Germany has such a high concentration of castles and nobles' estates in such a small space as the Münsterland. At one time there were said to be more than 3,000, the oldest of which date from the 13th century. The predominant architectural form was the moated castle; the landscape is too flat for hilltop castles, so buildings were sited in the middle of waterways or fortified by artificial dykes or ditches. They are often slightly off the beaten track. Many castles have been rebuilt several times over the centuries and today bear evidence of various architectural eras. However, buildings with a baroque slant are the most common, often in the Dutch baroque style. More than 100 moated castles can still be admired today, at least 40 of which are still in the possession of the aristocratic descendents of their original builders and the largest and most important of which is Schloss Nordkirchen, "Westphalia's Versailles." The castle rises on an islet fringed with magnificent French-style gardens. Another beautiful ensemble is the baroque Anholt Castle housing many treasures including a collection of Old Masters, and its parkland. Burg Hülshoff in Havixbeck near Münster was the birthplace of Annette von Droste-Hülshoff, Germany's most famous poetess, who immortalized Münsterland's moated castles in her work.

One of Düsseldorf's most spectacular pieces of architecture is Frank O. Gehry's Neuer Zollhof, with its projecting window-frame features. Further highlights are (opposite, from top) Benrath Castle; State governor's office and radio tower; carnival procession; and luxury boutiques along Königsallee. Top, from left: The River Rhine and its attractive villages are typical of the region. View from the Rhine Bridge at Wesel; city fortifications at Zons.

Düsseldorf and Lower Rhine

The capital of North Rhine Westphalia is a focus of fashion and culture, a major financial center and international trade show location. Königsallee, or "Kö," is a glamorous shopping street with exclusive fashion boutiques and designer stores. The Rhine region's cheerful good humor can be experienced over a glass of Altbier in the pubs and bars of the old quarter. But Düsseldorf also has a reputation as an important artistic and cultural city, with an array of art galleries and museums; Heinrich Heine and Joseph Beuys began their careers here. And then there's the Rhine, giving Düsseldorf all the flair of a waterfront city. Downstream from Bonn, the river is known as the Lower Rhine. Broad and majestic, fringed by low banks, it flows through Cologne, Düsseldorf, Wesel and Xanten to the northwest, finally passing the German-Dutch border at Emmerich.

Impressions of industrial culture: Zeche
Zollern pit (main picture, small picture
below left), Bochum Mining Museum,
pit frames at Zollverein and Nordstern
pits (top); gasometer in Oberhausen;
Meiderich Ironworks, a former wash-
room in the Mining Museum, and
Kokerei Zollverein (opposite).

MONUMENTS OF INDUSTRIAL CULTURE

The region between the rivers Lippe and Ruhr can look back on 150 years of mining and industry. Wherever coal was found above ground, it was mined as early as the Middle Ages. Not until the invention of steam power was coal mining able to move underground. This triggered the rise of heavy industry, which radically changed the face of the Ruhr district within a short space of time. For many generations, the pit frames, furnace towers and smoking chimneys were viewed as signs of economic prosperity. In 1970 a dramatic structural change began, as heavy industry declined in favor of service industries. Today, the remaining industrial buildings are museum-like memorials in a broad landscape devoted to leisure. The "industrial cathedrals" of iron and steel form a unique man-made landscape that brings the past to life. Disused pits still display their characteristic headgear, such as the famous Zeche Zollverein at Essen. In its day, this masterpiece of modern industrial architecture was known as the "finest mine in the Ruhr." The region is also home to former steel works with tall furnaces, such as Landschaftspark Duisburg-Nord, or the gasometer at Oberhausen, 116 m high and today offering magnificent panoramic views over the surrounding countryside. The gasometer is today a spectacular exhibition hall.

Lemgo Town Hall, a fine example of Weser Renaissance architecture, Schloss Corvey and monastery church with Romanesque westwork (top, from left). Bottom opposite: Schwallenberg in delightful Weserbergland, and Minden. Main picture: Externsteine rocks in Teutoburger Wald.

East Westphalia

Ostwestfalen (East Westphalia) is the name given to the northeasternmost tip of North Rhine Westphalia. Its most important cities are Detmold, Paderborn, Gütersloh, Bielefeld and Herford. It is bounded to the north by the North German lowlands and to the southwest by the Münster chalk basin. Teutoburger Wald (forest), a mountain gorge 100 km in length, was the scene of the Battle of the Teutoburg Forest (Hermannsschlacht) in 9 AD, where the Germanic forces conquered three Roman legions. The event is commemorated by the famous Hermann Memorial. The Externsteine rocks near Detmold and the Westphalian Open-Air Museum are also popular destinations. Lesser known but no less beautiful areas are the Eggegebirge mountains, bordering Teutoburger Wald to the south, the Wesergebirge to the east and Wiehengebirge to the west of Porta Westfalica.

The cathedral is Cologne's most central point of orientation, both from the opposite bank of the Rhine and from Roncalliplatz square (main picture and top, left). The church of St Martin (top right) is also well worth a visit. The old quarter offers many welcoming pubs (top, center).

Cologne

Germans quip that Cologne is ruled by the letter K: Kirchen (churches), Kunst (art) and Kölsch (the local beer). Today's metropolis on the Rhine grew from a Roman settlement. Declared an archbishopric by Charlemagne, Cologne was already a major German city in the early Middle Ages. Fascinating Romanesque and Gothic churches bear witness to the city's former significance as a spiritual and theological center; the most important is, of course, its most famous work of architecture, Cologne Cathedral. Art throughout the centuries is represented by a host of galleries – more than in any other city in Germany – and major museums including the Museum Ludwig or Wallraf-Richartz Museum. The joie de vivre of the Cologne people is legendary, and can be seen most clearly at carnival time – but not only then. Good humor is a part of everyday life for these Rhinelanders.

In addition to its Gothic cathedral, Cologne has many beautiful Romanesque churches, such as St Gereon (main picture). Bottom opposite, from top: the Römisch-Germanisches (Romano-Germanic) Museum, a reliquary bust in the Schnütgen Museum, and an altar painting in the Wallraf-Richartz Museum. Museum Ludwig (top left) has works from Old Masters to modern art.

CHURCHES, MONASTERIES AND MUSEUMS

As the seat of important bishoprics and a historical industrial region, North Rhine Westphalia also has many significant cultural treasures to offer. The most evident are the many Romanesque and Gothic churches, headed by the cathedrals of Cologne and Aachen, two of the world's finest works of religious architecture. Kloster Kamp, the first Cistercian monastery on German soil, was founded as early as 1123. The Corveyer Land region has around 22 monasteries and ruins, with Kloster Corvey as its primary attraction. Prosperous industrialists invested their profits in art and culture, such as Alfred Krupp, who built the classicist Villa Hügel in Essen, today used for traveling art exhibitions, or Peter Ludwig, whose modern art collection in Cologne bears his name. But the state and its municipalities also boast major museums of art and history, such as Cologne's Wallraf-Richartz Museum (art from medieval times to the 19th century), the North Rhine Westphalian Collection in Düsseldorf (classical modern art, Joseph Beuys) or the Römisch-Germanisches Museum in Cologne. Industrial heritage is recalled in museums such as the Mining Museum in Bochum or such cathedrals of industrial architecture as the machine house of the Zeche Zollern mine in Dortmund. The impressive art nouveau buildings house a museum.

Aachen's most important building is the Kaiserdom cathedral, with close links to Charlemagne – bottom left: bust of Charlemagne in Aachen's cathedral treasury; opposite, a portrait by Albrecht Dürer. The main picture shows the Emperor's throne. Top: exterior of the cathedral, its octagonal central chamber, the stained-glass windows in the choir, and the shrine.

Aachen

In the Middle Ages, Charlemagne's former residence was one of Europe's most important cities. The Romans had already established a settlement here because of its thermal springs, which were probably also the reason for Charlemagne's decision to expand the Aachen court into a palatinate over 1,200 years ago, in the winter of 794 to 795. Charlemagne, crowned emperor by the Pope in Rome in 800, died in Aachen in 814. In 936, Otto I was crowned King here, and the city was the place of coronation for the German kings until the coronation of Charles V in 1531. Even today, many historic works of architecture bear witness to this great era; these include the City Hall or the octagonal Pfalzkapelle chapel. The Cathedral was designated a UNESCO World Heritage site in 1978, and its treasury is the most important collection of church treasures north of the Alps.

Bonn is a city of culture, with sculptures by Niki de Saint Phalle (main picture). Opposite, from left: concrete sculpture "Beethon" in front of the Beethovenhalle and metal sculpture (Rheinisches Landesmuseum). Top: Schloss Augustusburg with stairway; dining-room in Falkenlust castle.

Brühl, Bonn

Bonn was Germany's capital for more than 40 years. Its Electoral Residence and Poppelsdorfer Schloss castle date from the baroque era. Bonn's City Hall is a graceful rococo building dating from 1738. The city's museum row along Adenauerallee and Friedrich-Ebert Allee includes the Bundeskunsthalle and Kunstmuseum (art), Haus der Geschichte (history) and Museum Alexander Koenig (zoology). The former government quarter inspires nostalgia, with the Bundeshaus (parliament buildings), "Langer Eugen" multistorey block, Villa Hammerschmidt and Palais Schaumburg. To the north of the city, Brühl is home to Schloss Augustusburg and Falkenlust hunting lodge. Augustusburg is celebrated as a masterpiece of rococo architecture, unfolding its full beauty when seen from the baroque gardens, designed by the French landscape gardener Dominique Girard.

Impressions of Sauerland, Siegerland and Bergisches Land: Burg Altena, the oldest youth hostel in the world (main picture), Freudenberg (top), Schloss Herdringen, bizarre rock formations in Hemer Felsenmeer, Haus Cleff in Remscheid-Hasten, and Schloss Berleburg (below, from top).

Sauerland, Bergisches Land, Siegerland

For the densely populated industrial areas on the Rhine and Ruhr, the extended mountainous regions in the south of North Rhine Westphalia have a twofold significance. Not only do their dams and reservoirs supply the region with water, but they are also a haven of unspoilt countryside for leisure seekers. The densely wooded Sauerland region, known for its many caves, has peaks up to 843 m in height in the Rothaargebirge mountains.

Even winter sports are possible here. To the south, Siegerland was an iron ore mining area for around 2,000 years anad is still an important ore processing center. Siegen was the birthplace of Peter Paul Rubens. The region, bordered by Bergisches Land to the west, is marked by forestry, animal husbandry and small-scale ore processing. Its cultural and economic center is Wuppertal, with its famous suspension railway.

The Moselle valley is Germany's oldest cultivated landscape. 2,000 years ago the Romans grew wine here, and began to cultivate the valley and set their stamp on the region. Below: the wine-growing village of Löf. Main picture: fairy-tale Burg Eltz castle high above a tributary of the Moselle. Dating from the 13th century, this fortress has been owned by the aristocratic Eltz family for 800 years.

RHINELAND PALATINATE, SAARLAND

Germany's southwest – the states of Rhineland Palatinate and Saarland – is a region of stark contrasts. The breathtaking cultivated landscapes along the rivers Rhine, Ahr, Nahe, Moselle and Saar border on Saarland's industrial region, today almost a museum, to form a strikingly attractive contrast. The area is rich in history, with many castles, churches and monasteries. And hedonists will be in paradise; thanks to the Romans – more wine is grown here than anywhere else in Germany.

Beautiful Eifel: Adenau, with its many half-timbered houses (top). Bottom, from left: Bertradaburg, Benedictine abbey of Maria Laach and Büresheim castle near Mayen. The 12th-century complex completely escaped destruction through the ages. Main picture: crater lake at Dauner Maare.

Eifel

"Eifel was everything rough and cold, sparse and poor, ancient in custom" wrote the poet Ernst Moritz Arndt in 1844. He describes the prejudices faced by the Eifel at the time, as an isolated "Rhenish Siberia." Perhaps the region did seem somewhat eerie; it is volcanic in origin. Hundreds of volcanoes shaped the landscape in the Daun and Manderscheid areas. The last major eruption was around 9,000 years ago, when particles of ash were carried as far as the River Elbe. Today, many craters have formed circular lakes known as "Maare". The Eifel region is among Germany's most beautiful mountainous areas, attracting plentiful visitors with its extensive forests, picturesque towns of half-timbered buildings, thermal springs, around 140 ruins, castles, palaces and monasteries, plus regional specialties and delicacies such as the fermented apple juice known as "Viez".

The European Grand Prix on the Nürburgring track is a mere home game for multiple world champion Michael Schumacher from nearby Kerpen near Aachen. He has celebrated many major wins here as part of the Ferrari team, with victories in 2000, 2001, 2004 and 2006. 2003 saw a different face on the winner's podium: his brother Ralf Schumacher.

NÜRBURGRING

Is it really the most famous racetrack in the world? True or not, it is certainly the most beautiful, and perhaps also the most challenging: Nürburgring. The circuit was built in the isolated wilderness of the Eifel at the end of the 1920s as part of an employment scheme, and was intended as a showcase for German automotive engineering and racing talent. It was later named "the green hell" in reference to its wooded environs. It takes its name from medieval Nürburg, which, like the villages of Quiddelbach, Herschbroich and Breidscheid, lies within the Nordschleife (North Loop) circuit. The legendary fame of Nürburgring as a Grand Prix track is a tapestry of triumph and tragedy, victory and defeat. In 1954, the Argentinian Onofre Marimón was killed here, and in 1976, Niki Lauda was involved in a crash and near-fatal fire. Formula 1 then moved to Hockenheim and did not return until 1995 – after Nürburgring had been modernized and shortened from 22.8 to 20.8 km – as the European Grand Prix. Nürburgring is a cult attraction, and not only for motor sports fans. In 2004, the 24-Hour-Race, an action-packed event full of thrills and spills, attracted more than 220,000 spectators – more than Formula 1. And every Whitsun weekend thousands of music fans attend the music festival, Rock am Ring.

Moselle highlights: the vine-flanked ruins of Burg Landshut near Bernkastel-Kues, summer residence of the Trier Electors (main picture). Top: the Imperial Thermae in Trier, the best-preserved Roman bathing complex north of the Alps. Ancient Trier had around 80,000 inhabitants and was one of the largest cities in the Roman Empire. Opposite, from top: loop of the Moselle at Bremm; Berg Castle at Perl-Nennig on the Upper Moselle (today a luxury hotel); Reichsburg castle at Cochem; river and vineyards at Leiwen.

Moselle Valley

The Moselle, Germany's most capricious river, is actually French, rising in deepest Vosges, meandering past Metz before reaching Luxembourg, and then entering Germany for the last 243 of its 544 km. More than 2,000 years ago, when Caesar conquered its length and the mountains around it, it was Roman and known as Mosella. Before that, the Celtic Treveri people, whose tribal capital was Colonia Augusta Treverorum, today Trier, had named it Mosea. The Moselle has more history than many another "German" river; Trier, Germany's oldest city, was founded on its banks. The Moselle courses past the steep terraced vineyards and castles for which the region is famous, a legendary beauty whose mellifluence, wine and rich fish stocks were already praised by the Roman poet Decimus Magnus Ausonius (310–395 AD).

Vintage Riesling matures in a wine cellar in Traben-Trarbach (main picture). Top, clockwise: in the cellar of winegrower Emil Franz in Traben-Trarbach; Heilsbruck monastery cellars on the German Wine Route; grape harvest above Traben-Trarbach; Riesling grapes; estate at Kallstadt.

FINE VINTAGES

Rhineland-Palatinate is grape-growing country. More wine is grown here than in any other region of Germany. The state encompasses six major growing areas: Ahr, Mosel-Saar-Ruwer, Mittelrhein, Nahe, Rheinhessen and Pfalz. Even that part of the River Saar known in good years for its legendary Rieslings flows through Rhine-land-Palatinate, joining the Moselle at Konz. Wine from this region has been the subject of many a story and song, many an author's work – and many a curse. Take the wine-sodden, inebriated tour-bus passengers along the Moselle, for example, or the "Wasserburgen" (water castles), the name given to ultra-large wine estates along the German Wine Route in the Palatinate. Or the story that the world's worst white wines come from here – but also the world's best. The latter is certainly true. The Rieslings from the Moselle, Saar and Ruwer, but also from the Nahe, Palatinate, Rheinhessen and Mittelrhein wine-growing regions, are experiencing an international renaissance, and some are doubtless among the best in the world. Red wines (Pinot Noir) from the Ahr, Pfalz and now Rheinhessen areas are also increasingly popular. Wine-growing in Rhineland-Palatinate is again approaching its heyday of the 19th century, when the great Rieslings of the region enjoyed legendary fame.

Romantic Rhine: Burg Stahleck castle at Bacharach (main picture). Top, from left: wine-growing town of Bacharach, Burg Rheinfels at St Goar, a river loop at Boppard. Below, from top: Mäuseturm (Mouse Tower) at Bingen; Pfalzgrafenstein toll castle and Burg Gutenfels at Kaub.

Middle Rhine

"I cannot divine what it meaneth" wrote poet Heinrich Heine about the Loreley, a rock 132 m high on the Rhine. A statement born in the yearning depths of the German heart – where romantic feelings revel. Here, in the Middle Rhine between Bingen and Koblenz, is the fount of German Romanticism. The glittering river meanders through a narrow valley past medieval half-timbered towns and mountain castles surrounded by vineyards.

Not only German hearts swell with sweetly melancholic nostalgia. Far and away the most beautiful stretch of the Rhine and a UNESCO World Heritage site, the region is among the most popular of all the world's travel destinations with tourists from Japan and the USA. The countryside is certainly glorious, and, when complemented by its fine wines, it is easy to fall in love with the Middle Rhine.

Nave of Worms Cathedral with baroque high altar by Johann Balthasar Neumann (main picture). Top: sandstone facades of Mainz Cathedral. Bottom: the six-spired Imperial Cathedral of Speyer with impressive crypt, its oldest section, completed in 1039 and consecrated in 1041.

IMPERIAL CATHEDRALS

The Imperial cathedrals on the Rhine are not only mighty works of architecture, but also important sites of German history. All three are in cities of Roman origin along the Rhine. Mainz Cathedral dates back to the late 10th century. The first version burnt down on the day of its consecration in 1009; its successor was built by Emperor Conrad II in the 11th century, and the present Romanesque cathedral by Emperor Henry IV Seven German kings were crowned in the Cathedral of St Martin and St Stephan. The Cathedral of Ss Peter and Paul at Worms was begun in the early 11th century. Conrad the Red, ancestor of the Salic dynasty, is buried here. Large parts of today's cathedral were constructed between 1130 and 1181. In 1147, St Bernard of Clairvaux gave the call to the Crusades in Worms Cathedral (his preachings here and in Speyer inspired many Germans to join the Crusades), and in 1521, Emperor Charles IV here imposed an imperial ban on Martin Luther. Majestic Speyer Cathedral is the largest Romanesque church in the world. Emperor Conrad II laid its foundation-stone in 1030. The crypt contains the tombs of four German kings, including Rudolf of Habsburg, and four emperors, including the unfortunate Henry IV who set off from Speyer on his penitential journey to meet the Pope at Canossa in 1077.

The Palatinate Forest is a paradise: forest meadows with violets and bluebells, the Teufelstisch (Devil's Table) rock at Dahn (top center). The loop of the River Saar at Mettlach (main picture) is one of its loveliest parts. By contrast, far right is Völklinger ironworks and industrial museum.

Palatinate Forest, Saar Valley

Two landscapes, two different regions, with little in common apart from geographical proximity. The Palatinate Forest belongs to the state of Rhineland-Palatinate, Saar Valley to Saarland. While the Palatinate and Saarland people take care to be neighborly, there is no love lost between them. The Palatinate Forest is regarded as Germany's largest continuous area of woodland, a paradise for hikers with countless castles and crags, and diverse flora and fauna. Even wildcats and lynx migrating from Vosges are believed to live here. The Saar Valley, however, has two faces – one industrial, one enchantingly natural. Between Saarbrücken and Dillingen are numerous (mostly disused) mines and ironworks; then the idyll begins and the lovely landscape of the region unrolls, reaching its high point at the loop of the River Saar at Mettlach.

Unchanged from 500 years ago when Luther was a student in Erfurt, the skyline of Thuringia's capital is still marked by its church steeples even today. Small picture: Mariendom cathedral, with Romanesque core, and, to its right, the Gothic Severi-kirche. Main picture: Reinhardswald forest to the north of Kassel is a popular excursion and houses Saba-burg Castle, made famous in the fairytale "Sleeping Beauty."

HESSEN, THURINGIA

These two states, once separated by the border between the two Germanys, are today the heart of Central Germany. Between the Rivers Rhine and Saale, between the Taunus, Harz and Thuringian Forest regions, is an area rich in idyllic nature – yet also an exceptional concentration of art and commerce, coupled with resounding names: Goethe's Weimar and Frankfurt's "Mainhattan," Luther's Wartburg, the art nouveau center of Darmstadt and Kassel, with its Documenta art festival – contrasts that could hardly be more exciting.

Main picture: Kassel Wilhelmshöhe rail and bus station. Left: Wilhelmshöhe castle; the sarcophagus of Henry the Lion and his wife in the Museum of Sepulchral Culture. Top: works by Yinka Shonibare, Kutlug Ataman and Fabian Marcaccio at the Documenta 11 modern art festival.

Kassel

Kassel's center was rebuilt in utilitarian style after World War II and has few attractions. But the Bergpark and Wilhelmshöhe castle, with its 70-m-high landmark, the Hercules Monument, more than make up for it. Museum Fridericianum was Germany's first public museum (since 1779), and has a famous collection of clocks and watches. Every five years (next due in 2012), the city on the River Fulda at the foot of Habichtswald forest is transformed into a parade of cutting-edge contemporary culture. The crème de la crème of visual artists from all over the world converge on Kassel, presenting their newest works at the Documenta international art exhibition. Infrastructure is also ultra-modern in the former capital of the Electorate of Hesse; Kassel-Wilhelmshöhe railway and bus station is a key transportation hub. The city has also gained in status as a business center.

The art of half-timbering can be found in many places, such as Homberg (main picture), Zwingenberg am Neckar, Michelstadt in the Odenwald or Miltenberg am Main (top, from left), but also in Bad Sooden-Allendorf on the Werra or Melsungen on the Fulda (bottom, from left).

HALF-TIMBERING

It's known from Japan to Oklahoma as the ultimate symbol of Germany's love of tradition and cosiness: the form of architecture known as half-timbering, where a framework of wood is infilled with clay, brick or masonry. Earlier versions of this form are documented in the pre-Christian Middle East and the Roman Empire, and in medieval times its popularity spread to England, Holland and Scandinavia. But the technique, involving joining a main beam known as a breastsummer to an upper framework by means of posts and studs with diagonal braces, reached its zenith in German-speaking countries. Oak was the wood predominantly used, but pine and spruce were also known. The construction and the patterns created by the wooden wall framework visible from both sides varied from region to region. Often, richly ornamented designs and carving can be found. In many areas the beams were dyed red with oxblood or black with tar, and the white interstices were faced with stippled plaster. Projecting upper stories were a characteristic feature of multistory burghers' houses. Half-timbering reached its heyday in the 16th and 17th centuries; many complete groups of buildings from this period can still be seen today in remarkable states of preservation, giving a vibrant flavor of the atmosphere of those times.

The ancient bishops' city of Fulda welcomes its visitors with impressive works of architecture. Its castle (below, bottom) and cathedral (top) were both built by the baroque architect Johann Dientzenhofer. But its many palaces, such as that on Friedrichstrasse (center), are also magnificent. The main picture shows the rotunda of the early Romanesque St Michael's Church, the small picture at the top is a study from Wasserkuppe mountain.

Fulda, Vogelsberg and the Rhön

Many millions of years ago, tectonic forces created striking natural rock formations in what is today the heart of Germany. Take Vogelsberg, around 50 km to the north of Frankfurt – in terms of area and mass, Europe's largest inactive shield volcano. With its mountain forests dotted with basalt crags and rolling park-like foothills, this leisure area is particularly popular with mountain bikers. A more austere but none the less captivating attraction is the Rhön region in the triangle between Hesse, Thuringia and Bavaria. Also volcanic in origin, it is composed of many single peaks and massifs. Two nature parks were established in this thinly populated area. Its highest mountain, the 950-m-high Wasserkuppe, is considered the birthplace of gliding, and is still a center of the sport. Numerous gliding events take place here during the summer months.

In addition to Limburg, the old university city of Marburg and the spa of Bad Ems, Wetzlar is a must for visitors to the Lahn Valley. The late Romanesque cathedral towers over Limburg (main picture and top), once the seat of the Supreme Court of the Holy Roman Empire. Top right: the Corn Market in Limburg. Below, from top: Wetzlar, Burg Greifenstein, Burg Runkel, the River Lahn in Nassau nature park.

Limburg and the Lahn Valley

One of the Rhine's most attractive offshoots is where the Lahn meanders between Taunus and Westerwald to its estuary south of Koblenz. Here, picturesque villages and towns, castles and fortresses rub shoulders. One of the brightest cultural jewels is the venerable bishops' city of Limburg on the border of Rheinland-Pfalz. It is overshadowed by the seven-towered late Romanesque cathedral of St George, built in the early 13th century and restored to its resplendent original colors. Linked to the cathedral and perched on the same chalk cliff falling steeply to the River Lahn below, is the castle, built by the Isenburg dynasty and dating back to the 7th or 8th century. The heart of the old town at the foot of this complex, particularly the area around the Corn Market, has beautiful half-timbered buildings with rich, often figurative carvings dating from the 13th to 18th centuries.

View of the Frankfurt skyline with 259-m-high Commerzbank Tower (main picture). In the heart of the city centre is the Platz an der Hauptwache with St Katharinen church; the Alte Oper (Old Opera) is the city's emblem (top, from left). But it's not all big business; "dolce far niente" also flourishes here. Warm evenings on the Museumsufer are a lively parade of seeing-and-being-seen; Sachsenhausen's cosy pubs (top right and below) serve the famous Äppelwoi cider.

Frankfurt am Main

The disproportion between the number of inhabitants and the city's financial clout is always astonishing. Although the old imperial city numbers only 660,000 people, Frankfurt is Germany's unequalled financial capital, home to Deutsche Bank and Commerzbank, Germany's most important stock exchange and a number of major insurance companies. No wonder the skyline of "Mainhattan," whose significance as an exhibition and stock exchange city has its roots in the 14th century, is bursting with confidence. In the shade of its skyscrapers, the other, older Frankfurt bravely maintains its position. It centers around the Römerberg, with the Römer, a group of buildings including the Old Town Hall, and the cathedral, where Germany's kings and later emperors were crowned. Paulskirche (church) was the scene of the first German national assembly in 1848 to 1849.

The market square of Michelstadt, with its late Gothic town hall (main picture). Top, from left: over 1,200 years old, the Torhalle (Gate Hall) of the Benedictine abbey of Lorsch; Gallery of Antlers at Schloss Erbach; the former castle at Michelstadt known as the "Kellerei"; Mittenberg am Main.

Odenwald

The Mittelgebirge mountain chain between the rivers Neckar and Main features wooded hills that pass into a monotonous plain to the east. In the south, however, the Neckar has carved a meandering and highly picturesque valley through the sandstone. At its northern edge, in Messel near Darmstadt, fossils excavated from the oil shale there are displayed in the museum, giving unique insights into the flora and fauna of 50 million years ago.

The region's rich history has left numerous castles and fortresses throughout the area, and ancient towns of half-timbered buildings. The main tourist attraction is Michelstadt, centrally located on the Nibelungenstrasse route. It is famous for its beautiful market-place with late Gothic town hall and for the Einhardsbasilika, a precious relic of Carolingian architecture. The beautifully preserved medieval city walls encircle the old city.

Two hundred years ago, the Wartburg (main picture) lay in ruins; it was rebuilt in Romantic style throughout the 19th century and again restored after 1945. Top, from left: Vogtei (bailiwick) with Nürnberger Erker oriel. Visitors' interest focuses on the room in which Luther translated the New Testament into German. The lower pictures show mosaics of St Elizabeth in the Elisabethkemenate (bower).

Wartburg

One of the outstanding symbolic buildings of German history, this castle complex to the southwest of Eisenach is said to have been founded in 1067 and was the ruling seat of the landgraves of Thuringia for many generations. It is claimed to be the site of the legendary minnesingers' contest (Sängerkrieg) held at the start of the 13th century and attended by Wolfram von Eschenbach, Heinrich von Ofterdingen and Walther von der Vogel-weide, which Richard Wagner portrayed in his opera Tannhäuser. In this period, the castle was inhabited by the Hungarian princess Elizabeth, later canonized for her work for the poor. First and foremost, Martin Luther, alias Junker Jörg, found sanctuary in the fortress under Elector Frederick III of Saxony when faced with the Imperial Ban and excommunication, and translated the New Testament into German in only 10 weeks in 1522.

"Erfordia turrita," many-turreted Erfurt, was the praise given by Martin Luther to this city on a ford of the River Gera, where he studied for four years. The etching by Wolfgang Taubert (top) shows Erfurt probably in Luther's time. Main picture: Cathedral and Severikirche.

Erfurt

Eleven monasteries, 21 parish churches, four collegiate churches and 15 monastery churches and chapels – as counted by diligent topographers – still tower over Erfurt's roofs today. The three-spired Mariendom cathedral is famous for its richly ornamented interior, including 15 High Gothic stained-glass windows and Romanesque Wolfram Chandelier. Together with the Severikirche, also with three steeples, it forms a most impressive backdrop – and not only when Erfurt celebrates the coming of spring with a lively fair. The half-timbered buildings of the Andreasviertel district and Krämerbrücke bridge, its stone arches fringed on both sides with houses, are equally memorable. Erfurt University was opened in 1392, the second oldest in Germany after Cologne, and in the early 16th century was a focus of humanism. It was closed in 1816 and reopened in 1994.

Weimar is overflowing with sites that immortalize the memory of its heyday: Goethe's and Schiller's houses, the German National Theatre and Herder church are among the most famous. Popular visitor attractions are also the City Castle with the "Red Salon" (main picture) and poet's chamber (picture below right) as well as the rococo Belvedere Castle (top). From October 2007, the Herzogin Anna Amalia Library and its magnificent rococo hall are also reopened following major restoration work after the extensive destruction by fire on 2 September 2004.

Weimar

The encyclopedia states that the small Thuringian city of Weimar became "a center of German intellectual life" after the mid-18th century. A stroll through its neat lanes today gives a flavor of the "genius loci" and clearly reveals its intellectual heritage. The city is rich in cultural monuments, and it is no wonder that much of it was designated a UNESCO World Heritage site. Of course, a major part of its fame is due to the two grandfathers of German classical literature, Goethe and Schiller, who once resided here. The centuries before and after also called forth numerous geniuses who contributed to the immortal reputation of the city, documented as early as Ottonian times: from Luther, Cranach and Bach to Franz Liszt, painters Böcklin and Liebermann, and the founder of the Bauhaus, Walter Gropius. Weimar, the city where culture is lived and breathed, was European Cultural Capital in 1999.

Goethe and Schiller before the National Theater, Weimar (main picture). Top: Auerbach's Cellar, which inspired Goethe to write the famous scene in Faust. Opposite: Goethe's summerhouse on River Ilm, Juno Room and library in Goethe's house, parlor in Schiller's house, and house exterior.

GOETHE AND SCHILLER

When talk turns to Weimar, those interested in modern German history may recollect the Constitution passed in August 1919 by the National Assembly in the theater of that city. However, a brighter light was shed on Weimar by Anna Amalia in 1772. The duchess from the Braunschweig dynasty had appointed the poet Christoph Martin Wieland as the court tutor for her princes, and soon collected a literary circle around her in the Wittumspalais and Schloss Tiefurt. Soon the duchess son Karl August called Johann Gottfried von Herder and Johann Wolfgang von Goethe to Weimar. Friedrich Schiller followed in 1799. These great poets and thinkers together founded the Weimar Circle, bringing their chosen home to fame as the center of German classicism. Yet it was the latter two who rose to become the main inspirations of Weimar's flourishing cultural tourism today. The main destination for pilgrims is, of course, Goethe's house at Frauenplan, where the privy councilor lived for 47 years. The simple baroque building is still furnished today as it was then – with antique-style elements and the "ultra-modern" furnishings of the time. Schiller's house in Schillerstraße has authentic furnishings of the period. The homes of these two literary giants seem to be awaiting the imminent return of their owners. Here, time seems to have stood still.

Study with toadstool in the Thuringian Forest (main picture). Top, from left: Sonneberg Toy Museum; hall in the Renaissance castle of Wilhelmsburg; fascinating stalactites and stalagmites in the Fairy Grottoes near Saalfeld. Below: loop of the River Saale at Bad Lobenstein.

Thuringian Forest, Saale Valley

The Thuringian Forest, Germany's geographical center, and the Schiefergebirge mountains to its southeast form the country's largest continuous forested area. The two mountain chains, up to 1,000 m high, were already popular summer destinations in Goethe's time, thanks to their rolling countryside and balmy climate. Pretty spas and health resorts, an extensive network of walking routes and outstanding winter sports opportunities have significantly increased their tourist attraction since then. Meiningen, Bad Salzungen, Bad Liebenstein, Oberhof and Schmalkaden, with its listed old quarter, or Schmiedefeld am Rennsteig, on the well-known ancient hiking trail that follows the traditional boundary between Northern and Southern Germany – equally popular with summer and winter sports fans – are only a few of the excursion destinations in this largely unspoilt region.

An immense artistic and cultural heritage can be found between Naumburg and Magdeburg. Moritzburg hunting castle is an extremely popular visitor attraction (below). The main picture shows a section of the famous Fürstenzug (Procession of Princes), a portrait gallery of the House of Wettin. The porcelain frieze, on the outer wall of the Langer Gang walk in Dresden, is over 100 m long.

SAXONY-ANHALT, SAXONY

If Berlin is the reunited Republic's modern heart of power politics, the two states of Saxony-Anhalt and Saxony are its historic origins. Between the Harz and Erzgebirge regions and the rivers Neisse, Elbe and Saale are ancient cities, churches, monasteries, castles, estates and forests, with countless breathtaking artistic treasures. The population in this richly historic area is young, and many opportunities are opening up in the region, which is also noted for its stunning landscapes and diversity of leisure facilities.

Magdeburg is at the eastern edge of the fertile Magdeburger Börde plain in the middle reaches of the River Elbe. A focal point of the city panorama is St Mauritius Cathedral (main picture). Top: the ruling couple enthroned in a chapel of the cathedral probably represent Emperor Otto I and his wife Editha; cathedral ambulatory. Stendal and Tangermünde are ancient Hanseatic cities; their landmarks are the statue of Roland at Stendal Town Hall and the Stephanskirche church in Tangermünde (opposite, bottom).

Magdeburg and the Middle Elbe

Magdeburg, former Hanseatic city and today the capital of Saxony-Anhalt, has been an important center of traffic since the Middle Ages, not least because of its harbor on the River Elbe. It is also renowned as a center of industry and research, notably the famous experiment by Otto von Guericke using the "Magdeburg Hemispheres" to demonstrate air pressure and a vacuum. However, the historic significance of the city, already documented as a trading center in the Carolingian era, is outstanding. As early as the mid-10th century, Emperor Otto I chose to reside mainly in Magdeburg, whose constitution, or Magdeburg Law, was applied in many more newly founded cities. In addition, he declared it an archbishopric in 968. This move opened the city as the starting-point for the Slav missions and colonization of the East. Damaged in World War II, its center was modernized in 1990.

In 1800, after 35 years, the Wörlitzer Anlagen gardens were finally completed. The 112-ha grounds, with exotic flowers, shrubs and trees, also conceal many fascinating buildings. These include Wörlitz Castle, in its beautiful location, a superb example of classical architecture (main picture and below). In keeping with the romantic spirit of the time, they were intended to recall the Prince's travels in Italy and England. The Gothic House (top) was built from 1773 in neo-Gothic style.

Wörlitz

Halfway between Dessau and Wittenberg is the region's largest and most popular attraction: the world-famous gardens of Dessau-Wörlitz. In 1765, "Father Franz," as Leopold Frederick Franz von Anhalt-Dessau was affectionately known by the people, commissioned Germany's first landscaped gardens, to be laid out in the English style on Wörlitz Lake. Shortly after, the prince's summer residence was completed on the banks of the lake, designed by the architect Wilhelm von Erdmannsdorf and the first major classical building in the country. Now a museum, the castle contains the prince's extensive collection of art, and its well-preserved interior conveys an authentic feel of princely living. The gardens also contain a host of other fascinating buildings, in addition to grottoes, temples and picturesque nooks. They were designated a UNESCO World Heritage site in 2000.

The colorful town hall in Wernigerode is a jewel of the Harz region's half-timbered architecture (main picture). St Servatius collegiate church and the Renaissance castle tower over Quedlinburg, whose old quarter is a UNESCO World Heritage site (top). Left: half-timbering in Quedlinburg; bottom: Quedlinburg market square.

Quedlinburg, Wernigerode

Quedlinburg, in the northern foothills of the Harz, is more than 1,000 years old and a rare architectural jewel. In the early 10th century, two settlements were founded here on the banks of the Bode under the protection of the Imperial Palatinate of Henry I, the Saxon duke and first German king. The settlements soon merged into a town, where a monastery was founded and market, coinage and customs privileges conferred. "Quitlingaburg" soon developed into a center of commercial and cultural life, joining the Hanseatic League in 1426, and has retained its medieval atmosphere. Wernigerode, to the west, is equally picturesque; the chief treasure and unique emblem of this richly colorful city is its town hall, more than 500 years old, with two slim oriel towers and magnificent facade. A narrow-gauge railroad runs from Wernigerode to the Brocken mountain.

The town hall and St Mary's Church today dominate the marketplace, with statues of Luther and Melanchthon; left, a portrait of Luther by Cranach. Top: at Luther's house in Collegienstrasse; far right interior of the castle church. Bottom: the church tower and famous doorway.

Luther's City of Wittenberg

Wittenberg, on the north bank of the River Elbe and the southern offshoots of the Fläming, is, as its official subtitle makes plain, inseparably linked to the great reformer Marin Luther (1483–1546). Luther came to the city in 1508 as an Augustine monk and taught theology and philosophy from 1512 at the local university, founded ten years previously by Elector Frederick the Wise. Luther sparked the Reformation in October 1517 when he nailed his famous 95 theses challenging clerical misrule to the church door. Many buildings in the city associated with this event have been declared UNESCO World Heritage sites. Wittenberg honors its greatest son with a memorial on the marketplace, in front of the town hall and St Mary's Church. Other famous scions of the city were the painter Lukas Cranach the Elder and the theologian and scholar Philipp Melanchthon.

George Frederick Handel presides over the marketplace of Halle, before St Mary's Church and the Red Tower. Naumburg's attraction is its late Romanesque early Gothic cathedral (large picture, right), with the world-famous sculptures of its founders (bottom right). Bottom left: cemetery on the River Saale. Top: the Renaissance castle of Bernburg on the Saale.

Halle, Naumburg and the Saale Valley

The catchment area of the Rivers Saale and Unstrut, with its vineyards, impressive castles and fortresses, museums and wide-ranging sporting activities, is an attractive destination for excursions and leisure-seekers. Halle has been the region's main city for more than 1,000 years. This former Hanseatic city, which amassed early riches from salt mining, was a major industrial center during the era of the German Democratic Republic. A remarkably large proportion of the medieval and Gründerzeit (late 19th century) period architecture has been well preserved. George Frederick Handel, Halle's illustrious scion, gave the city on the edge of the Harz region and the Leipzig basin its outstanding reputation as a city of music. Naumburg lies amid vineyards to the south of the confluence of Unstrut and Saale. It is principally famous for the twelve statues of its founders in the cathedral, dating from 1250.

The "capital of reunification" and second largest city in the "new German states" (former East Germany) also played a key role in Goethe's life and work. Top, from right: the poet drew inspiration for the famous scene in "Faust" from Auerbach's Cellar, probably Germany's most famous inn. Goethe's statue stands in front of the Alte Börse (Old Exchange) on the Naschmarkt; the city's first baroque building from the late 17th century. Main picture: the glass-roofed Neue Messe exhibition center. Bottom: view of the Gewandhaus concert hall, built 1981.

Leipzig

Almost 1,000 years old, this city on the Weisse Elster river, the end of the German Democratic Republic was formalized in 1989, has long presented a many-faceted image to the world. As a city of books, for example: it is the founding city of such major publishing houses as Baedeker and Brockhaus, and headquarters of the German Libraries Commission. In terms of music, it was home to Bach, Mendelssohn and Schumann and today boasts the Thomaner Choir and Gewandhaus Orchestra. Leipzig also saw the foundation of the General German Workers' Association by Lassalle in 1863. The city has Germany's second oldest university after Heidelberg (1409) and is a flourishing industrial center. But its main claim to fame since the late Middle Ages is as an exhibition center. The symbol of this unbroken tradition is the gigantic glass center built in the mid-1990s – the Neue Messe.

Dresden's old city was irrevocably destroyed at the end of World War II. However, many of its most famous buildings, principally the Zwinger palace (below), Semperoper (top left), Residence Palace and Hofkirche church (top right) and the elegant Brühlsche Terrasse promenade curving around the River Elbe (main picture) have been lavishly rebuilt.

Dresden

"The Venice of the East," "Saxon Serenissima," "Florence of the Elbe," "Pearl of Baroque" – the epithets given to the capital of the Free State of Saxony over the years are as numerous as they are effusive. And with good reason. The former Electoral Residence is without a doubt one of Europe's greatest cultural metropolises. Ruling seat of the Albertine dynasty since 1485, in the 17th and 18th centuries Dresden grew into one of the most magnificent baroque residential cities in Germany under the auspices of Augustus the Strong and his successors. In the late 18th and early 19th centuries, bourgeois intellectuals made Dresden a center of German Romanticism. However, the devastating bombing of February 1945 spelled doom for the glorious city; its old quarter was completely destroyed. After a mammoth reconstruction program, the city's magnificence can once again be experienced.

Dresden's skyline is once more complete: in 2005 the Frauenkirche church returned to dominate Dresden's Neumarkt (New Market Square). Designed by Georg Bähr, the church was built between 1722 and 1734 and is considered one of the finest Baroque protestant churches in Germany. Top: a Veduta (view) from 1748 by the painter Bernardo Bellotto. Below right: The cupola of the Art Academy and behind it the unique dome of the Frauenkirche, famed as the "Stone Bell", one of the greatest buildings of its kind north of the Alps.

THE DRESDEN FRAUENKIRCHE

This building dominated the skyline of "Saxony's Serenissima" until it was razed in February 1945. Today, after its ceremonial consecration in October 2005, it is an impressive celebration of the Dresden people's will to rebuild. It is, of course, the Frauenkirche, whose unique dome, known as the "Stone Bell," is once again proudly reflected in the River Elbe. As early as the 11th century, a mission church of Our Lady stood on the site, but after 700 years and much conversion, the original church was found to be too small and dilapidated. In 1722 the decision was made to rebuild from scratch, to designs by baroque architect George Bähr, and a monumental 95-m-high central nave with five galleries was erected, crowned by a mighty dome 23.5 m in diameter. Immediately after World War II, the plan of reconstructing "Germany's most important ecclesiastical building" was mooted, but not until after reunification were concrete steps taken by a citizens' action group, supported by the city and Saxony's state church. Bähr's brilliant design was gradually reconstructed at enormous cost and effort from the original plans. Original stonework and pieces of the original altar were salvaged and incorporated, and old painting and building techniques were recreated to ensure the maximum authenticity.

Impressions of the Elbe: Pillnitz Castle (main picture), Meissen with cathedral, and Albrechtsburg, and Elbe castle at Albrechtsberg (bottom). Meissen became famous for its "white gold" – Europe's first hard porcelain, produced since 1710 in the Meissen works founded by Augustus the Strong and exported all over the world to this day, with its distinctive mark of crossed cobalt-blue swords.

Upper Elbe Valley

Broad river meadows, forests, vineyards, parks and gardens, and picturesque towns such as Pirna and Radebeul (home of Germany's famous author Karl May), magnificent castles such as Moritzburg, Seusslitz, Pillnitz or Albrechtsburg… the Saxon Elbland region is rich in cultural treasures. Meissen is a historic focus. "Saxony's cradle," where the German emperors once founded the first settlement on Slav soil, was the residence of the Wettin dynasty in the 12th century and preserved its medieval atmosphere throughout World War II. The historic old quarter, with its marketplace and half-timbered buildings is still overshadowed by the representatives of spiritual and secular power, visible from far and wide: the Gothic Cathedral of St John and St Donatus, and the Albrechtsburg, original site of the porcelain factory, housed in the late Gothic castle of the Wettins.

Main picture: the Basteibrücke bridge links the mighty crags of the Bastei. Small picture below: magnificent view of the Elbe Valley from the rocky turrets of the Bastei. Top, from left: Neurathen cliffs and two landscapes in the Elbsandsteingebirge mountains.

Saxon Switzerland

The region known as Saxon Switzerland is one of Saxony's most delightful excursion destinations. Covering 360 sq km in the Elbe sandstone mountains, this nature reserve continues beyond the Czech border. The best impression of the hundreds of bizarre rock formations fringing the meandering river valley to the southeast of Dresden, is gained from a river cruise; but the roadway also offers glorious views of the deeply cleft plateaus, with enchanting scenery that has not only thrilled generations of romantically minded tourists, but also inspired Richard Wagner to write "Lohengrin" and Carl Maria von Weber to compose "Der Freischütz". The Basteibrücke bridge, leading 200 m from Neurathen Castle to a viewing platform "floating" above the Elbe, affords a breathtaking view over river and rocks. The fortress of Königstein is also a major tourist attraction.

A treasure-trove of knowledge is the Oberlausitz Library of the Sciences in Görlitz, a city noted for its exceptionally rich architectural heritage (main picture). Top: Rathausplatz square in Zittau, in the triangle between the Czech Republic and Poland. Its neo-Renaissance town hall was designed by Schinkel. Opposite, from top: meadows at Stolpen, east of Dresden; baroque monastery of Marienthal on the River Neisse near Görlitz, St Michael's Church and Old Water Tower on the banks of the Spree at Bautzen, and the garden of a half-timbered house typical of the Lausitz region.

Lausitz

The Lausitz, a region near the Polish border bounded by the rivers Elbe and Oder, Spree and Neisse, is home to the Sorb people, an ethnic minority today numbering around 60,000. The Lusatian and Milcane peoples, Slavic in origin, outlived the German movement to colonize the east, and their descendants have retained their unique culture and language. While the Niederlausitz region, to the south of Cottbus and largely within the state of Brandenburg, is marked by pine forests and extensive lignite and open-cast mining, the Oberlausitz to the northeast of Saxony is known as "Land of a Thousand Lakes." Large areas of its picturesque heaths and wetlands, with 5,000 km of walking trails, were declared a UNESCO Biosphere Reserve. The Grenzwall border area between Ober- and Niederlausitz is undergoing extensive natural regeneration.

Automotive history, from Horch and Audi to the Trabant, can be seen in Zwickau's Automobile Museum (main picture). Bottom: department store facade; industrial museum in Chemnitz. Top: winter on Fichtelberg mountain; nutcrackers, incense burners and all kinds of wooden toys have a 300-year tradition in the Erzgebirge mountains.

Zwickau, Chemnitz and the Erzgebirge

The Erzgebirge, a mountain chain on Saxon and Bohemian ground and up to 1,200 m high, has remained an area of enchanting natural beauty despite acid rain and the depredations of centuries of intensive mining. The basin to its north, however, has always been known for its industry. Its heritage is rich and varied: in the Industrial Museum in Chemnitz, for instance, a city known in the 19th century as "Saxony's Manchester" and "Sooty Chemnitz" and later, for 37 grey years, as Karl Marx City; or in the Automobile Museum in Zwickau, the home of such wheeled legends as Horch, Wanderer, DKW and Trabant. Chemnitz today is reflected in the glassed facade of its department store, designed by top architects Murphy/Jahn. The center has been remodeled in recent years, and now new architecture sits side by side with historic buildings such as the 12th-century Red Tower.

The Stuttgart summer residence of Duke Carl Eugen of Württemberg is named, surprisingly, Solitude (small picture). It was known for its glittering festivals once praised by Casanova himself. Magnificent rococo: the 11th-century Benedictine abbey of Wiblingen near Ulm was completely rebuilt from 1714 to 1781. The library from 1744 is one of Germany's most impressive rococo buildings, with a glorious ceiling fresco and symmetrical columns.

BADEN-WÜRTTEMBERG

Although known as the "Ländle" or little state, Baden-Württemberg, created as late as 1952 from the former states of Baden, Württemberg-Baden and Württemberg-Hohenzollern, is in fact an economic powerhouse and rich in cultural and natural beauties. The region has Germany's highest density of scientific, academic and research organizations. It offers ancient cities, castles and fortresses, monasteries and churches. And the spirit of poets and thinkers is still in the air; Frederick Schiller is just one of its many great scions.

Impressions of Romanticism: Heidelberg by night, with Brückentor gate and Heiliggeist-kirche church (main picture). Top: Castle ruins; monument to Perkeo, the elector's dwarf jester and a prodigious drinker. Large picture on right: View of Heidelberg. Opposite, from left: Karzer (university lock-up) and Brunnenhalle with Friedrichsbau castle.

Heidelberg

Although actually the historical capital of the Pfalz (Palatinate) region, today Heidelberg belongs to Baden-Württemberg, a matter for much dismay among Pfalz natives. With its old quarter, castle and location on the River Neckar, it has remained the capital of German romanticism. The Counts Palatine selected the beautiful city as their residence. In 1386, Rupprecht I founded the university and began to expand the castle, which later served as the seat of the Electors Palatine. It was the birthplace of Liselotte of Pfalz, who married the Duke of Orleans. The hereditary title claims raised by the French as a result of the marriage triggered a war; the castle was destroyed in 1688 to 1689 and in 1693, and the Counts Palatine moved their residence to nearby Mannheim. Yet Romanticism lives on in Heidelberg, and it is wellknown as a place to lose one's heart.

Idyllic River Neckar landscapes in the former imperial city of Neckargmünd (main picture). Top, from left: ducal residence in Ludwigsburg and the rococo palace, Favorite. Bottom, from left: Hirschhorn, Zwingenberg Castle, Bad Wimpfen with Kaiserpfalz palace, banks of the Neckar at Tübingen.

Neckar Valley

Watching the river flowing so gently and calmly, it's hard to believe its name, of Celtic origin, means "wild water". Tamed by 27 barrages, it flows through the "little state" for 367 km, rising in the eastern Black Forest foothills near Villingen-Schwenningen. Like almost all Germany's rivers, the Neckar has shaped the culture of its region; the land on its banks was made cultivable and cities were founded that rose to become seats of political, economic and intellectual power – such as Stuttgart, Ludwigsburg, Heilbronn, Bad Wimpfen, Eberbach, Hirschhorn, Neckargmünd and Heidelberg. One of the most beautiful – and even today a stronghold of German philosophy – is Tübingen, the "pearl of the Neckar," with its university dating from 1477, the birthplace of Ludwig Uhland and last home of Frederick Hölderlin, as well as many famous scholars of international renown.

Views of Stuttgart: the Wilhelma, the Zoological-Botanic Gardens, with Moorish palace (top). The classicist State Gallery (main picture) has paintings and sculpture from the 14th to 20th centuries. Opposite, from top: the famous Kunstmuseum, the fountain on Schlossplatz, and Schillerplatz, with its monument to the prince of poets.

Stuttgart

The capital of the state (population: 590,000) has a very special charm, between dynamism and nonchalance, and between industry, culture and pleasure. Mercedes and Porsche build the world's finest automobiles here, the art and culture scene is famous throughout Europe, and the "wine capital" has 400 hectares of vines to ensure that everyone "gets a drop." The city's name comes from Stuotgaden, meaning "mares' garden," and refers to a stud farm belonging to the Alemannic duke of Liutolf in the 10th century. In the 14th century Stuttgart was first the residence of Württemberg's counts, later its dukes. From 1805 to 1918, the city was the capital of the Kingdom of Württemberg. Today it is the center of world-famous company Daimler Chrysler. And at the Cannstatter Wasen fair, it is also the center of Swabian exuberance, when the hard-working people lets their hair down.

Like a fortress, the mighty three-spired Minster of St Stephan (12th–14th century) towers over the city of Breisach from its perch on a hill over the Rhine (main picture). Below: Rhine water-meadows in Taubergiessen. Top, from left: Interior of Rastatt Castle, built between 1697 and 1707 in the Versailles style by "Turkish Louis," Margrave Ludwig Wilhelm; three-winged Residence with extensive grounds.

Upper Rhine

Baden is also the hazy sweep of the Upper Rhine plains, bordered by the Black Forest to the east and Vosges to the west. It is an ancient transit route, traversed by Celts, Romans, Alemanni, Burgunds and Franconians. A battle lasting several centuries was waged over the question of whether the Rhine really was the border between Baden (in other words, Germany) and France – and how German or how French was neighboring Alsace? This key issue overshadowed the development of cities such as Breisach (founded by the Romans as Mons Brisiacus), Rastatt, once the residence of the Baden margraves, or Karlsruhe, built from the drawing-board in 1715, fanning out from the castle of Margrave Karl Wilhelm of Baden Durbach. Today Karlsruhe is the seat of the German Constitutional Court and the Federal Supreme Court. It is also a center of technological and scientific study and research.

The Gothic minster of Freiburg is the city's landmark, built from 1200 as a tomb for the family of Duke Berthold V of the Zähringen dynasty (below). Top, from left: Schwabentor gate, Colombi palace and facade of the Gothic Kaufhaus (Merchant's Hall) on Münsterplatz square.

Freiburg im Breisgau

Like an exclamation mark, the 116-m-high Gothic spire of Freiburg Minster towers high above the university city. It is even visible from Vosges, in competition with Strasbourg. The clear-cut, elegant and almost playful filigree design of the cathedral must have rubbed off on the mentality of the Freiburg people. Freiburg is believed to be the sunniest city in Germany, and its charming atmosphere is infectious. Here life is for pleasure, and art and wine in particular. The city was founded in 1120 by the Zähringen dukes, and developed into an important cultural center. The magnificent old city went up in flames in the bombings of World War II, but was later restored. During much of its history – from 1368 to 1806 – Freiburg belonged to the House of Habsburg, and thus to Austria. Perhaps this era is responsible for the people's nonchalant air, with their motto of "take things easy."

Main picture: A panoramic view across the vineyards covering the lowlands of the upper Rhine Valley near Ebringen, south-west of Freiburg im Breisgau. Below right: The picturesque village of Ortenberg is dominated by the castle of the same name (13th century), rebuilt in the 19th century in neo-Romanesque style and today a youth hostel. Adjacent: Idyllic Ettenheim in the southern Ortenau region, with baroque Church of St Bartholomew. Above: Rötteln castle in the Markgräflerland region near Lörrach, close to the Swiss border.

BADEN'S WINE ROUTE

"Baden's wine – blessed by the sun" is the slogan of the region's wine growers. And it's true. Baden has the highest summer temperatures in Germany; spring comes earlier here, and golden autumn often continues well into November. Its a region that's ideal for wine and the people who enjoy it. Wine is grown in almost every area of the state. In the Neckar and Rems valleys and their offshoots, to the north in Taubertal, at Lake Constance, but above all on the Rhine, on the west-facing slopes of the Black Forest, in Kraichgau and along the Badische Bergstrasse route. The 160-km-long Baden Wine Route winds through the most beautiful areas of Baden's vineyards (around 16,000 ha of vines in total), beginning in Baden-Baden and heading south through picturesque Ortenau and Breisgau, past Kaiserstuhl and Tuniberg into the tranquil rolling hills of Markgräflerland, Germany's Tuscany. The route is marked by hosts of pretty villages and towns, and many marvelous wines: crisp, zesty Riesling and elegant Gewürztraminer, full-flavored Pinot Blanc and Gris (Weiß- and Grauburgunder), characterful Pinot Noir (Spätburgunder) and smooth Gutedel, a Markgräflerland speciality – a fascinating journey of discovery and delight. The region's specialties are designed to perfectly complement its wines, with hearty delicacies.

The Hexenlochmühle at St Märgen (main picture). Opposite: peak of Hornisgrinde mountain, waterfalls at Bad Rippoldsau – Schapbach, Black Forest house in Gutach valley, stream at Hexenlochmühle. Below: vintage cars in Baden-Baden, colonnade at Trinkhalle (Pump Room), bower in the Rose Garden. Top: Cistercian monastery in Maulbronn, fountain hall and frescoes.

Northern and Central Black Forest

"God's pharmacy" is the name given to the Northern and Central Black Forest by its inhabitants. But "Fairytale Land" or "Gourmets' Paradise" would be equally accurate. Nowhere else in Germany is there such a concentration of relaxing health spas; the mountain air and numerous thermal springs promote health, and in the enchanted valleys and villages imagination can still conjure up many a character from legend and fable. And Gourmets' Paradise? What a question! The food in this part of the Black Forest, where the (Michelin) stars also shine by day, is second to none in Germany – savory, yet sophisticated. And that brings us to Baden-Baden, a city that, as the name Baden (bath) suggests, focuses on health, yet with a few irresistible venial sins – gambling (in the Casino or at the Iffezheim horse-racing track) and wine (everywhere).

Top picture series, from left: Laufenburg and St Fridolinsmünster in Bad Säckingen. Right picture series, from top: View from Hohen Belchen mountain, Feldsee Lake, an upland pasture on Gaisberg mountain and Lotenbachklamm, a ravine in the Wutach Gorge (also main picture).

Southern Black Forest and Hochrhein (High Rhine)

In the Southern, or High, Black Forest, the woods are especially dark, with some peaks topping 1,000 m. Home to spicy-scented pinewoods, mountain valleys and lakes, rushing torrents, more or less isolated farmhouses – and Black Forest Cherry Cake. Home to winter sports meccas such as Hinterzarten and monasteries such as the Benedictine abbey of St Blasius. Now and again visitors encounter a natural phenomenon such as the "Black Forest's Grand Canyon," the Wutachschlucht gorge. Or bask in the tranquility at the peak of Hoher Belchen (1,414 m) or Feldberg (1,493 m), where chamois graze. Further south at the lower edge of Hotzenwald forest, the Hochrhein forms the border with Switzerland, with romantic towns like Bad Säckingen, Laufenburg and the twin town Waldshut-Tiengen, set in wonderful walking and hiking country with plentiful marked trails.

Austere and full of character: the countryside of the Swabian Alb and Danube gorge (main picture). Opposite, from top: Lichtenstein castle over Echaztal valley, waterfall at Bad Urach, smithy at the Blautopf, a 21-m-deep water source, and Sigmaringen Castle.

Top, from left: Rare birds of the Alb. The kingfisher fishes only in crystal-clear streams and rivers; the owl hunts in lonely forests; the jackdaw often makes its nest in castle towers. Storks and herons can also be found. Fauna include badgers, foxes and wild boars.

Swabian Alb and Danube Valley

The Swabian Alb is a geologically unique mountain range. Chalk and limestone formations have created karst caves. The limestone uplands above the lush valleys have karstified into bare heaths with grasses, wild herbs and juniper over which shepherds still drive their sheep. The stone is so porous that the Danube, the official source of which rises in a stone basin in Donaueschingen, partly disappears into the ground at Tuttlingen, rising again nearby to cleave through steep cliffs. The region has been designated a UNESCO Geopark for its fascinating geology. The Swabian Alb was settled as early as the Stone Age. In medieval times, some famous castles were built here including Sigmaringen, still today the seat of the Hohenzollern dynasty that once ruled over Prussia and all Germany, and Haigerloch, Heidenheim and the fortress of Lichtenstein.

View from Neutorbrücke bridge to Ulm Minster: The Gothic church (built from 1377) dominates the skyline (main picture). Opposite, from top: Minster interior in late Gothic style. Particularly beautiful are the magnificent choirstalls (1469–1474) by Jörg Syrlin the Elder and Michael Erhart.

Top: picturesque skyline of Ulm with the Danube and patricians' houses in the old quarter, the Minster towering behind them. The legend of the Tailor of Ulm recounts his attempt to launch a flying-machine from the Minster, only to land ignominiously in the Danube.

Ulm

The old saying "Venetian power, Augsburg magnificence, Nuremberg humor, Strasbourg arms and Ulm money rule the world" says it all. Ulm on the Danube, originally Hulma or "marshy spot," and a free Imperial city from 1274, played an important role in the late Middle Ages. Thanks to its location at the junction of key trade routes, it became a center of textile trading. The power once held by the weavers and merchants is impressively recalled today by the masterfully restored buildings of the old quarter, above all the city hall from 1370, with its exquisite, bright painted facade. Around 1500, Ulm was Germany's second largest city after Nuremberg. Its monumental Minster, visible from afar, still makes the Danube city unique today. The Gothic steeple from which the Tailor of Ulm launched his attempts to fly is the highest in the world, at 161,53 m.

The celestial realms of late baroque: the Library in Bad Schussenried monastery (main picture). Cherubs in Zwiefalten Monastery (immediately below). Top, from left: frescoes in Bad Wurzach castle; frescoes in St Martin's Church, Biberach. Opposite, from top: ceiling of Gutenzell church with frescoes by Johann Georg Dieffenbrunner; ceiling of St Martin's Church, Biberach; ceiling of collegiate and parish church in Bad Buchau.

Upper Swabia

Upper Swabians may be famous – or infamous – for thrift that borders on miserliness, but their churches celebrate abundance. Upper Swabia (southern Württemberg to Lake Constance) is thus synonymous with the baroque era. This was partly due to the prosperity of the parishes and monasteries, but also because baroque was a means of propaganda for the Catholic Church against its Protestant rival, a kind of Counter-Reformation adver-

tising campaign. The bright and sensuous baroque style was intended to lure people back to the "right" faith. Posterity can thank the clergy's machinations for a wealth of sacred treasures, such as the monastery and church at Zwiefalten, Schussenried monastery and Steinhausen pilgrimage church. The latter is said to be the most beautiful village church in the world – if, indeed, it is fair to draw comparisons.

Images from the Alemannic "Fasnacht", or carnival. Top, from left: "Schrättele" mask from Bad Waldsee; two "Fasnet" masks in Schramberg. Main picture: "Narrensprung" (Fools' Leap) parade in Rottweil on Carnival Monday and Shrove Tuesday. Over 1,000 "fools" gather from 8 am. Opposite: carnival masks in Rottweil and Elzach.

FASNACHT – CARNIVAL

The name is actually "Fasnet," not "Fastnacht" or "Fasching" and certainly not "Carnival," if the Swabian and Alemannic version is meant. Unlike carnivals in Mainz, Cologne or Dusseldorf, which developed as a protest against French occupation under Napoleon, Fasnet has pagan roots. Ethnologists believe it originated in pre-Christian vegetation cults intended to repel demons inimical to growth and attract the benevolent spirits of spring. And many masks and costumes are certainly more frightening than funny. Carnival obeys a strict ritual presided over by carnival guilds. Essential elements are the costume ("Häs") and mask ("Scheme"). These masks are often elaborately carved and handed down from generation to generation. Witches with evil expressions and long broomsticks are also terrifying. Other figures crack long whips or create a deafening row with wooden rattles and metal bells. Almost every town and village in Baden and Upper Swabia has its own carnival event, with Rottweil probably the most traditional. Festivities are generally at their height in the week up to Ash Wednesday, from "greasy Thursday" to Shrove Tuesday, with elaborate parades and processions. Since rivers of alcohol also flow, the stage is set for carnival passion, with flirting behind the masks the order of the day.

Picturesque views: Meersburg Castle with view of the lake; here the poetess Annette von Droste-Hülshoff lived and died (main picture). Right: baroque among vineyards – Birnau pilgrimage church and its magnificent baroque interior. Below, from top: Romanesque collegiate Church of St George, an emblem of Reichenau monastery island; reconstruction of the 4,000-year-old pile dwellings in Unteruhldingen; delightful Montfort Castle in Langenargen.

Lake Constance

Let's start with some figures about the "Swabian Sea": 64 km in length (Ludwigshafen to Bregenz), 14 km at its broadest point (Friedrichshafen to Romanshorn), deepest point (upper lake) 250 m, area 540 sq km, circumference 255 km, volume 55 billion cub m of water. Otherwise the lake is a matter for poets and romantics, who fall into paeans of praise at the ensemble of water, picturesque villages, the Alpine scenery, silken air and sweeping blue sky in good weather. The feeling is unmistakable: The South starts here. In bad weather, it has a certain mystery that inspires the imagination. Lake Constance is a luxury to enjoy every day. And that has been its attraction for more than 4,000 years – from the earliest lake-dwellers to present-day German author Martin Walser, with his poet's workshop in Wasserburg.

Nymphenburg Palace in Munich was built by Ferdinand Maria, Elector of Bavaria, in the mid-17th century to celebrate the birth of the heir to the throne, Max Emanuel. It epitomises the harmony of baroque architecture.

Seeon Monastery in Chiemgau features a variety of architectural styles. Baroque master builders added onion domes to the Romanesque towers, while the interior is Gothic (main picture).

BAVARIA

The "Free State of Bavaria" can boast landscapes unique in all of Germany – from the river valleys of the Main and Danube to the Alpine peaks at Garmisch-Partenkirchen or Berchtesgaden. Countless palaces, castles, monasteries and churches also bear witness to the region's cultural and political history. The Bavarian people are known for their zest for life and close bonds with tradition, and perhaps for this reason have retained a profound awareness of their ethnic and national independence.

The wine-growing village of Eschendorf, high above the River Main (main picture). Opposite, from left: St Maria pilgrimage church near Volkach; altar of St Bartholomew in Volkach. Top, from left: the moated castle of Mespelbrunn in Spessart; Johannisburg Renaissance castle in Aschaffenburg.

Spessart, Mainfranken

The River Main forms the historical and economic lifeline of the Mainfranken (Main Franconia) and Spessart regions. Between West Spessart and the eastern Steigerwald forest, the river meanders alongside steep slopes, many covered with vineyards, and later passes through ever-broadening valleys. The river has created a timeless cultivated landscape of exceptional charm, which wine connoisseurs will be happy to confirm – it is also the home of the special flagon-shaped "Bocksbeutel" bottles of Franconian wine. Why not combine a visit to one of the picturesque wine-growing villages along the Main with a wine tasting session? But the region has more to offer; it was the home of great artists including Tilman Riemenschneider and Johann Balthasar Neumann, whose masterpieces of sculpture and architecture can be admired in Volkach or Würzburg.

The almost Mediterranean silhouettes of St Kili-an's Cathedral and the Neumünster and Marien-kapelle churches dominate the city's skyline. In the 18th century, 12 larger than life-size figures of saints were added to the Alte Mainbrücke, a late Gothic bridge dating from 1133 (right). It's worth taking a look underground, too; marvel at the old wine cellars of Juliusspital (opposite).

Würzburg

Largely destroyed in World War II, today this university town on the River Main, beautifully located at the foot of Marienberg fortress and the city vineyards, again has a charming Old Quarter. It extend around the Market Square, with its late Gothic Marienkapelle church and Haus zum Falken, with ornate rococo stuccowork. The city's numerous hidden treasures include Lusamgärtlein, behind the baroque Neumünster church, the burial place of the medieval troubadour Walther von der Vogelweide. But the high point of a visit to Würzburg must be the magnificent Imperial Residence (1720), a baroque masterpiece declared a UNESCO World Heritage site in 1981. Built by the architects Lukas von Hildebrandt and Johann Balthasar Neumann, it also houses a breathtaking staircase with ceiling frescoes by Giambattista Tiepolo.

Würzburg Residence is a collection of architectural superlatives. The glorious interior of its Hofkirche church (main picture) is adorned by cherubs and stucco marble. Further masterpieces in the Residence (opposite, top to bottom) are the Tiepolo self-portrait in the staircase ceiling frescoes, the staircase itself, the Hofkirche from a different perspective, the Mirror Cabinet and the Green Salon. Adjacent: Balthasar Neumann had himself immortalized in colonel's uniform on the cornice of the staircase ceiling frescoes. Top: view of the Residence from the gardens.

WÜRZBURG RESIDENCE

Würzburg's historic seat of the prince-bishops of the Schönborn family is an outstanding masterpiece of baroque architecture, the equal of Versailles and the Habsburgs' palace of Schönbrunn in Vienna. Awarded World Heritage site status by UNESCO in 1981, the Residence was begun in 1720 as a commission by Prince-Bishop Johann Philipp Franz von Schönborn to the master builder Johann Balthasar Neumann, then aged 33. It would prove to be his masterpiece – a work of true genius. Influenced by master builder Maximilian von Welsch and Vienna architect Johann Lukas von Hildebrandt, its design combines baroque elements of style from throughout Europe, yet is the most homogeneous and extraordinarily creative of all the baroque palaces. The Residence is set in magnificent rococo-style gardens dating from the 18th century. The most significant feature of the interior is the immense staircase. Its three flights are spanned by a spectacular painted ceiling by Giambattista Tiepolo, the largest continuous fresco in the world (1751 to 1753) and considered the high point of his artistic career. At the heart of the Residence is the magnificent Kaisersaal; other treasures include the restored Hall of Mirrors and Green Salon and the Court Church at the southwestern corner wing – all outstanding works of Franconian rococo.

Bamberg is an almost completely intact historic city, with a skyline dominated by the Gothic cathedral and mighty St Michael's Monastery on Michelsburg hill (main picture). In the 14th century, the inhabitants of Bamberg chose an unusual site for their town hall – an artificial island in the River Regnitz (top). The Knight of Bamberg (opposite) is a famous statue from the 13th century.

Bamberg

The ancient imperial and episcopal city of Bamberg, more than 1,000 years old, spans seven hills in the valley of the River Regnitz. Unlike Nuremberg or Würzburg, this former "caput orbis" (capital of the world) suffered only minor damage in World War II, and still retains all the atmosphere of an old print. For this reason, Bamberg was designated a World Heritage Site in 1994 and, with its Old Quarter and world-famous orchestra, it has plentiful attractions, including the Old Town Hall (14th century), the old fishermen's quarter of "Little Venice" and the late Romanesque cathedral with the "Knight of Bamberg." The Imperial Tomb in the interior was carved by Tilman Riemenschneider between 1499 and 1513, and the Altar of Mary is by Veit Stoss. The western choir houses the only papal tomb in Germany (Clement II); the Diocesan Museum displays the cathedral's valuable treasures.

One of Europe's most beautiful baroque theaters is the Margravial Opera House in Bayreuth (main picture and below). Other jewels in the city (upper row, from left) are the Hermitage, the New Palace (shown: a statue in the gardens) and the Sun Temple crowned with a figure of Apollo.

Bayreuth

Bayreuth is primarily associated with Richard Wagner; indeed, the two names have been almost synonymous since the composer built his famous festival theater here in 1872, supported by his patron King Ludwig II. Every year, international fans of Wagner attend the Wagner Festival, with its distinguished opera performances. But Bayreuth has more to offer. Margravine Wilhelmine, favorite sister of Frederick the Great, created a city in the style of Bayreuth rococo, extending the Eremitage, Old and New Palaces and the magnificent Palace Gardens from 1736 onward. The Margravial Opera House, a masterpiece of European baroque, was also founded on her initiative. Its opulence inspired Richard Wagner to come to Bayreuth after his plans for a festival theater in Munich had failed, although his Ring cycle was performed there only once in his lifetime due to financial tribulations.

Impressions of medieval Nuremberg: the unique half-timbered buildings at the foot of Kaiserburg fortress at Tiergärtnertor Gate (main picture). Top: Maxbrücke bridge over the River Pegnitz, with old wine depot and Hangman's Bridge. Bottom, from left: the world-famous Christmas market; the ornate clock on the gables of the Frauenkirche church.

Nuremberg

Nuremberg people love life, their beautiful city, their beer and their famous finger-size sausages – both hot from the grill with fresh sauerkraut, and as "saure Zipfel" in a tangy, vinegary sauce. At the Christkindlesmarkt in winter, mulled wine and nutty, spicy Nuremberg Lebkuchen are popular. Life is there to be enjoyed in Albrecht Dürer's home city, perhaps because the former Free Imperial city was once one of Europe's major art and trading centers. Visitors alighting at the main station immediately face the medieval city walls with Frauentor gate. The mighty Kaiserburg palace was the scene of many historical events. Impressive churches such as Lorenzkirche, with the "English Greeting" by artist Veit Stoss, or Sebalduskirche, with Peter Vischer's Sebaldus Tomb, and stately burghers' houses are witnesses to Nuremberg's great history.

St Coloman pilgrimage church against the backdrop of Schwangau Mountains (main picture). Nearby are Neuschwanstein Castle (below right) and the Wieskirche church, built by Dominikus Zimmermann with interior by his brother Johann Baptist (top row). Donauwörth, with Gothic church and 15th-century Tanzhaus (below left).

ROMANTIC ROAD

Occasionally, nature and civilization complement each other so perfectly in a landscape that we experience the beauty of a vision in our waking moments. Rare though these experiences are, the Romantic Road offers a rich succession of them. A journey along this route is steeped in history, with a millennium of history reflected in its towns and cities, its monuments and art treasures. The Romantic Road leads south from Würzburg through the Tauber Valley, past the picturesque cities of Rothenburg, Dinkelsbühl and Nördlingen. Nestled in the rolling hills along the Danube rise the roofs and towers of Donauwörth. The prospect broadens, now only framed by the Alps to the south. A series of magnificent churches and castles stand picture-perfect in the countryside. The artists who created the rococo churches of the Pfaffenwinkel (Priests' Corner) region between Schongau and Füssen brought heaven down to earth; just look at the pilgrimage church of St Coloman, or the Wieskirche at Steingaden. The Romantic Road finally ends in the Alpine foothills at Füssen. But before this, travellers are rewarded with a final crowning moment as the turrets of Neuschwanstein, the fairy-tale castle built by the "fairy-tale king," Ludwig II of Bavaria, come into sight only a few hundred miles from the road – an enchanting vision of beauty.

Rothenburg ob der Tauber is a jewel of late Gothic architecture. Quaint crooked lanes link squares each more romantic than the last. A few highlights are the Rödertor gate (main picture), the city skyline, Market Square, Plönlein (little square) at Schmiedgasse and the Town Hall (below, from top). Top: these saints' figures can be seen in Jakobskirche.

Rothenburg ob der Tauber

Rothenburg ob der Tauber is the epitome of German romanticism. When films call for scenes from the Middle Ages, Rothenburg often serves as the backdrop; its medieval charm has survived almost intact. Praised by painter Ludwig Richter as "a fairy-tale of a city," Rothenburg transports visitors into another age with its unique ensemble of red roofs, towers and turrets, town hall, sweeping market square, fountains, city gates, churches, plentiful half-timbered buildings and 2 km of city wall. Visitors interested in finding out more can explore the museums offering in-depth insight into medieval times, including the Reichsmuseum, with a beer stein dating from the Thirty Years' War, plus exhibitions and reconstructions of medieval interiors, or the Medieval Crime Museum, showing the darker side of medieval life and a history of law and justice.

The Befreiungshalle (Freedom Hall) at Kelheim, with its 34 winged victories, was built by Leo von Klenze (main picture). The Danube Gorge (Donau-durchbruch, top); the interior and a detail of the rococo abbey church in Weltenburg (below). Below right: rococo library of Metten Monastery.

Lower Bavaria, Danube Valley

Of the many outstanding sights in Lower Bavaria, one of the most beautiful is the Danube Gorge at Weltenburg, where the river carves its way through towering limestone cliffs. The Danube is Lower Bavaria's most important lifeline, its banks lined with cities and monasteries such as the Benedictine monastery of Metten (766) famous for its magnificent library. Weltenburg Monastery (around 600) is Bavaria's oldest abbey. Its baroque church is a masterpiece by the Asam brothers. Only a few miles down the river is Kelheim, with the Befreiungshalle, built 1842 to 1863 in memory of the Wars of Liberation against Napoleon; the city of Straubing farther to the east was founded by the Romans. Lower Bavaria's capital is Landshut, where the spectacular Landshut Wedding pageant is celebrated every four years. Many of the locals don traditional costumes for the occasion.

The historic city of Passau (top left) on the peninsula between the rivers Inn and Danube forms a glorious ensemble, dominated by the towers and cupolas of Stephansdom, the most important Italianate baroque church in Germany. Main picture: From a more western perspective: Stephansdom and St Paul's are the most striking features. In the foreground are the Danube Quays with cruise ships. Top: one of Regensburg's oldest monuments is the 310-m-long Stone Bridge which has spanned the Danube since 1135.

Regensburg, Passau

Two of Germany's loveliest cities are medieval Regensburg, with its cathedral, old salt depot, city gates and Stone Bridge, and Passau, "pearl of the baroque". Regensburg was a Celtic settlement, then became a Roman military camp. In 739, St Bonifatius established an episcopal see. From 1245, the Free Imperial City rose to become Southern Germany's most prosperous city and seat of the Imperial Diets. Passau, too, can boast 2,000 years of history. Founded on the confluence of the rivers Danube, Inn and Ilz and originally a Roman camp and fortress, in 735 Passau became the seat of a bishopric extending as far as Hungary. As the residence of the supreme prince-bishopric, Passau became an important trade center. Italian architects were commissioned in the 17th century to rebuild the cathedral and gave the city its present baroque appearance.

Where the wild waters flow – the Höllbachg'spreng Falls at Großer Falkenstein to the east of Zwiesel (main picture). Winters are long in the inclement Bavarian Forest, which is often covered with snow well into spring. Opposite: in the Bavarian Forest National Park, wildcats, brown bears, lynx, wolves, hares and many other animals can be seen wild or in enclosures.

Bavarian Forest

A mysterious wood, wild and full of secrets, tales and myths, with deep-rooted traditions and ancient crafts almost forgotten elsewhere; a place where glassblowers and other artisans can be watched at their work. But the greatest charm of the Bavarian Forest is its still remarkably unspoilt landscapes. Mountain woods, moors, granite and gneiss crags, Alpine meadows, lakes and rivers form a unique natural setting, described in spellbinding detail in the works of the 19th-century author Adalbert Stifter. The Mittelgebirge mountain chain, with peaks of up to 1,457 m (Grosser Arber), is a paradise for hikers and cross-country skiers. The Bavarian Forest National Park is a fascinating primeval forest where nature has been left to itself – even where the woods have been devastated by the bark beetle – to create landscapes often bordering on the surreal.

Lindau's Gothic and baroque old quarter opens onto the lake port, with its lighthouse and Bavarian lion emblem (main picture). Lindau is the only Bavarian city on Lake Constance (Bodensee), whose banks lie primarily in the Baden-Württemberg region, Austria and Switzerland. The glorious evening atmosphere at Forggensee artificial lake near Füssen is set off by the Tannheimer Berge mountains (top). Below: Lindau Town Hall, built 1422 to 1436.

Lindau, Upper and East Allgäu

The Allgäu region is (largely) part of Bavaria, even though the language is rather different. While the Swabian-Alemannic dialect points to the different origins of the people, the picturesque Alpine landscape, the baroque churches, the ancient cities like Lindau, Kempten, Memmingen, Kaufbeuren or Füssen and the mentality of their inhabitants all indicate that the Allgäu is part of Bavaria. The region is generally associated with lush green meadows and mountain pastures where cattle graze, and it is in fact Germany's leading cheese producing area. The peak of the Allgäuer Hauptkamm offers magnificent views of the captivating landscape. Lindau has an almost Mediterranean air. Once a Free Imperial City that fell to Bavaria only in 1805, it is enchantingly sited on an island in Lake Constance and connected to the mainland by two bridges.

Towering ina spectacular location on a crag at the foot of the Ammer Mountains near Füssen is the "fairy-tale castle" of Neuschwanstein (top). Main picture and below: Ludwig II had the Throne Room designed in Oriental style, with cobalt-blue Moorish pillars and ornately decorated arches. Bottom right: "Fairy-tale King" Ludwig II, from a painting by Franz von Piloty.

NEUSCHWANSTEIN

When the morning mists lift, Neuschwanstein Castle rises from the East Allgäu Alps like a mirage. The castle was actually inspired by the dreams of Bavaria's King Ludwig II, who planned it as his Grail castle. In 1869, he commissioned the castle to be built to designs by theater scene painter Christian Jank. In neo-Romanesque style, it replaced the ruins of Vorder-Hohenschwangau and was modelled on Wartburg near Eisenach in Thuringia – the setting for Wagner's opera "Tannhäuser." Obsessed by Wagner, Ludwig sought salvation in his retreat of Neuschwanstein just as the opera figure of Tannhäuser did in the Venusberg. Ludwig II commissioned the finest artists and craftsmen of the time to design the interior, placing no restrictions on style; frescoes show scenes from Wagner's operas, while the throne room is inspired by the Hagia Sophia in Istanbul. Ludwig II spent no more than a few days at Neuschwanstein; here he was arrested and overthrown, for reasons including the immense building costs he was incurring, and the region's accompanying debts. Ludwig died under mysterious circumstances, found drowned in nearby Starnberg Lake in 1886 at the age of 41. Today, Neuschwanstein is one of the most popular castles in the world, and Bavaria has reason to be grateful to Ludwig for this lucrative attraction.

Augsburg's former wealth is evidenced by its Renaissance town hall and adjacent Perlach Tower (main picture). Top: the Golden Hall in the town hall, with magnificently ornamented ceiling. Opposite: the Schätzlerpalais with Rococo Hall and (bottom middle) statue of Jakob Fugger.

Augsburg

Augsburg is a divine city, for it owes its existence to the goddess Cisa. Swabian peoples between the Rivers Lech and Wertach had established a shrine to the goddess, which developed into the settlement Cisaris and then became the Roman military camp Augusta Vindelicorum in 14 BC – making Augsburg Germany's second oldest city after Trier. It blossomed as a major center of trade between the Orient, Italy and Southern Germany in the 15th and 16th centuries. The history of Augsburg is inextricably bound up with the Fuggers, a family that founded the greatest bank and one of the richest trading dynasties in the world. Jakob Fugger "the Rich" (1493–1560) and his descendants were important patrons of the arts and art collectors; the city today owes many magnificent buildings and parks to them in addition to the world's oldest social housing settlement, the Fuggerei.

Nymphenburg Palace (main picture). Top: the many-towered Munich skyline with Frauenkirche Cathedral, St Peter's Church, the city hall, the Holy Spirit and Theatiner churches. Below, from left: Siegestor arch, Feldherrnhalle, Theatiner Church, the cathedral with city hall, and statue of Bavaria.

Munich

Munich is the capital of Bavaria – but the joie de vivre of the city tells us a different story: Munich could be Italy's northernmost city. Its architecture, coupled with the op-timistic, positive attitude of Munich people, creates an almost Mediterranean ambience. Henry the Lion is regarded as the city's founder; he established a salt route across a lucrative toll bridge near the monastery settlement "at the monks," which later became the name Munich. In the 13th century, the city became the residence of the Wittelsbach dynasty, and was capital of the Duchy (later the Kingdom) of Bavaria from 1506. In the 19th century, King Ludwig I embarked on an ambitious building programme and founded Munich's reputation as a city of the arts and sciences. Add to this Bavaria's glorious blue skies and unique beer-garden culture in warm weather – and you have a city with distinctive flair.

The classical Königsplatz square, with the Propylaea, is home to the Glyptothek, with its famous collections of antique statuary. Munich has a rich array of theaters and museums: the Cuvilliés-Theater and Opera House (top, from left), sculpture by Olaf Menzel in the Pinakothek der Moderne, the Barberini Faun in the Glyptothek, Old Masters in the Alte Pinakothek, aircraft in the Deutsches Museum, vintage wheels in the BMW Museum (left, from top).

ART AND CULTURE IN MUNICH

Where savoir-vivre is a way of life, art is never far behind. And so Munich is Germany's second metropolis (after Berlin) of the fine arts, which were also supported by the Wittelsbach dynasty throughout their reign. The city has several world class orchestras – such as the Munich Philharmonic and the Bavarian Radio Symphony Orchestra – and a first-class opera house in the Nationaltheater. Munich is legendary for the diversity of its theater landscape, the most famous being the Münchner Kammerspiele, the Residenztheater, Staatstheater am Gärtnerplatz, Prinzregententheater, Volkstheater and the Cuvilliés-Theater in the Residence. Germany's most beautiful rococo theater, it was built 1751 to 1753 by Francois de Cuvilliés. Munich is also a city of museums; its best known is probably the Deutsches Museum, the country's most important science and technology history museum. But the Alte Pinakothek, the Neue Pinakothek and the Pinakothek der Moderne are also museums of international repute, spanning all eras of art from medieval times to the present day. Further major museums are the Haus der Kunst with visiting exhibitions, and the Lenbachhaus with a permanent exhibition of the "Blue Rider" movement. Outstanding modern buildings in the city are the Olympic Stadium and the new "Allianz-Arena" football stadium.

A visit to the Munich Oktoberfest or "Wiesn" is a very special experience (main picture and below). Top, from left: less bustling temples of hospitality are the Chinese Tower beer garden and the Hofbräuhaus, with live brass band music daily.

BEER AND PRETZELS

When Munich's joie de vivre overflows, it's often because of the beer. Munich is known as the most famous city of beer in the world. Every year, millions of visitors from all over the world travel to Munich, "home of the Hofbräuhaus," as the song goes. Not only because of the city's six great breweries, but also because the Munich calendar revolves around beer. Early spring is the "strong beer" season, followed by Maibock in May and the beer-garden season in summer – when the Chinese Tower in the English Gardens, one of the city's many such hostelries, becomes one of the best places to make new friends. And finally, there's the peak season – the Oktoberfest, the largest fair in the world. Its Theresienwiese site becomes home to a real city with up to half a million "inhabitants" per day, with beer tents seating up to 6,000 people each, all celebrating the two-week festival with beer, grilled chicken and pretzels. And don't forget the Hofbräuhaus, the world's most famous beer hall, a rustic paradise where Americans, Australians, Italians, Japanese – and real Munich people! – collect to drink the health of Germany's feel-good factor, "Gemütlichkeit," accompanied by the world-famous toast "Oans, zwoa, gsuffa" (one, two, down the hatch!). It's easy to get into conversation with somebody and make new friends.

A golden morning – the sun rises over one of the Osterseen lakes south of Starnberg Lake (main picture). At Andechs Monastery on the hill at Ammersee, visitors can enjoy a Doppelbock beer and experience the "Andechs feeling" (top). Opposite, from left: the memorial cross in Starnberg Lake marks the spot where King Ludwig II drowned; an evening concert in Benediktbeuern Monastery, the oldest in Bavaria, founded in 730, is among the many pleasures of this part of Upper Bavaria; sublime mountain scenery unfolds at Sylvenstein Reservoir.

Five Lakes Country, Isar and Loisach Valleys

The magic of this region to the south of Munich, irrespective of the time of day or year, is quite simply enchanting. One of the most breathtaking experiences is to watch the sun rise or set over one of the lakes – free of charge, and priceless. The lakes in Five Lakes Country are Starnberger See, Ammersee, Pilsensee, Wesslinger See and Wörthsee. Each has its own distinctive character and atmosphere, and together they form one of Bavaria's most beautiful natural spectacles. The Isar rises in the Austrian Karwendel Mountains as a rushing torrent, but is soon tamed in Sylvenstein Reservoir. At Wolfratshausen, it flows through the unspoilt floodplain of the Pupplinger Au. The River Loisach also rises in Tyrol; from Kochelsee it meanders through moorlands to the Beurer Moos and Mondscheinfilz plains before meeting the Isar at Wolfratshausen.

Main picture: on a clear day, the view from the Zugspitze (here with Schneefernerhaus and weather station) extends to the Bohemian Forest. Top, clockwise: impressions from the Alpine foothills – a spring meadow, Karwendel Mountains with Lautersee, chapel on Wendelstein. Bottom, from left: house murals in Unter- and Oberammergau, farmhouse in Bad Tölz.

Bavarian Alps

Bavaria is a land of mountains. And by "mountains" Bavarians generally mean the Alps, the mountains of their homeland. Like Switzerland, Austria, France, Italy and the Principality of Liechtenstein, Bavaria is an Alpine region. A section of the Alps around 400 km long – but a mere 20 km wide – stretching from west to east lies within Bavaria's borders, divided into Allgäu Alps, Ammergau Alps, Wetterstein Mountains, Bavarian Alps, Karwendel, Berchtesgaden Alps and Chiemgau Alps. The highest peak, and thus Germany's highest mountain, is the Zugspitze, at 2,962 m. The beautiful mountain landscapes and picturesque foothills, together with the numerous mountain lakes – like Königssee, Walchensee, Spitzingsee, Schliersee and Tegernsee – attract many thousands of tourists plus active winter and summer sports fans to Bavaria every year.

The hills of Chiemgau, carved by the Ice Age, gently enfold the banks of Lake Chiemsee. The White Fleet steamers await their passengers at the pier at Gstadt, on the lake's northern banks (main picture). The heart of Herrenchiemsee castle is its magnificent Hall of Mirrors (top). The staircase, for which only the finest artists and craftsmen of the time were commissioned, is hardly less impressive (below).

Chiemsee

Chiemsee is the "Bavarian Ocean," Bavaria's largest lake (not counting the Bavarian part of Lake Constance). Created by melting glaciers, the lake is 80 sq km in area and up to 74 m deep. Its banks are partly overgrown with reeds and are gradually silting up. A boat tour of the lake is a popular visitor attraction in the summer. In the lake are two islands, Herrenchiemsee and Frauenchiemsee, on which monks and nuns founded religious settlements as early as the 8th century. The main attraction is the castle of Herrenchiemsee, built from 1878 on the order of King Ludwig II. He planned a castle as magnificent as that of his great idol, the French "Sun King" Louis XIV. However, only the central block was erected; finances were exhausted before the wings could be built, and work stopped completely in 1886. The king himself spent a mere nine days in his "Versailles."

What a beautiful region! Main picture: Hochkalter mountain from Lake Taubensee. Right picture series, from top: View from the Jenner over cloud-covered Lake Königsee to the Watzmann; the Schleierfälle waterfalls; picturesque Ramsau with its late Gothic church. In winter, Lake Hintersee, at the foot of the Reiter Alpe mountain (top), is enchanting.

Berchtesgadener Land

Sometimes beauty can be a painful sight – for instance, when it oversteps the boundaries of kitsch. But how exactly to define kitsch in relation to beauty? Nature can never be kitsch, and the views in Berchtesgadener Land are perfect natural compositions, an interplay of mountains, forests, lakes, clouds, sky and the human element, adding buildings that harmonize with the scene like artists' inspirations in a picture. The calm, fjord-like lake of Königsee and pilgrimage village of St Bartholomä with its famous echo, the mighty Watzmann, which claimed so many would-be conquerers of its north face, the mountain village of Ramsau with its delightful church, the venerable saline and health spa and resort Bad Reichenhall, and Berchtesgaden nestled in the mountains, with its royal palace, historic salt mines and museums. Definitely Bavaria at its most beautiful!

Romanesque and Gothic on the banks of the Rhine: The mighty four-square tower of Great St Martin and the two spires of Cologne Cathedral, 156 m high and the highest church towers in the world at the time of their completion in 1880, dominate the surrounding buildings in Cologne's old quarter. Cologne offers a host of art and culture in addition to Kölsch beer, carnival and churches.

ATLAS

Germany can be divided into three geographical regions: the North German lowlands, the Mittelgebirge mountains and the Alps, with their foothills. The country measures a maximum of 876 km from north to south and 640 km from west to east. With a total area of 357,023 sq km, Germany is not particularly large, so that its attractive opposites are never far away from each other: bustling metropolises and rural idylls, 1,000-year-old cultural monuments and high-tech industrial works, flat plains and high peaks.

Munich's football stadium, the Allianz Arena, designed by Herzog & De Meuron, is the world's largest membrane shell construction, with a total of 2,760 air-filled "cushions." Of these, 1,056 can be lit up in red, blue or white, depending on the team playing.

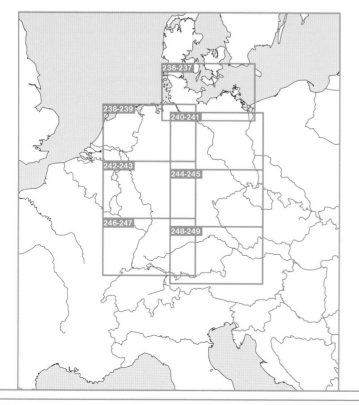

KEY TO MAPS
1 : 950,000

═══════ ⋯⋯	Autobahn (freeway, motorway) (under construction)
═══════	Toll autobahn
═══════ ⋯⋯	Highway with four or more lanes (under construction)
═════ ⋯⋯	Interstate highway (under construction)
════ ⋯⋯	Major highway (under construction)
═════	Highway
════	Subsidiary road
┅┅┅┅	Railroad
────	Restricted zone
────	National and nature park
4 2 A22	Autobahn number
E54	European highway number
34 28 N22 66	Other highway number
══22══	Autobahn junction number
━━●━━	Junction
🚍	Unsuitable for caravans
✖	Caravans prohibited
⊙	Autobahn fuel station
⊗	Autobahn service area
⊠	Autobahn service area with motel
✈	Key airport
✈	Airport
✈	Airfield
⛴	Car ferry

KEY

The maps on the following pages show Germany to a scale of 1: 950,000. Geographical and geological details are complemented by an array of tourist information in the form of a detailed road network and pictograms showing the location and type of all key attractions and leisure destinations. Cities and towns with sights and attractions of interest to tourists are highlighted in yellow. UNESCO World Heritage sites in the various categories (cultural, natural/geological, biosphere reserves) are marked.

PICTOGRAMS

- Auto route
- Rail road
- Shipping route
- UNESCO World Heritage (Natural)
- Mountain landscape
- Extinct volcano
- Rock landscape
- Ravine/canyon
- Cave
- River landscape
- Waterfall/rapids
- Lake country
- National Park (fauna)
- National Park (flora)
- National Park (landscape)
- Nature park
- Biosphere Reserve
- Coastal landscape
- Zoo/safari park
- Botanic gardens
- Fossil site
- Wildlife reserve
- Protected area for sealions/seals

- Island
- Beach
- Spring
- UNESCO World Heritage (Cultural)
- Remarkable city
- Pre- and early history
- Roman antiquity
- Places of Jewish cultural interest
- Places of Christian cultural interest
- Romanesque church
- Gothic church
- Renaissance
- Baroque
- Christian monastery
- Vikings
- Cultural landscape
- Castle/fortress/fort
- Palace
- Technical/industrial monument
- Memorial
- Space telescope
- Historical cities and towns
- Impressive skyline

- Festivals
- Museum
- Theater/theatre
- World exhibition
- Olympics
- Monument
- Tomb/grave
- Market
- Theater/theatre of war/battlefield
- Remarkable lighthouse
- Remarkable bridge
- State Historical Park
- Visitor Center
- Disused mine
- Castle ruin
- Tower of interest
- Windmill
- Remarkable building
- Motor sport track
- Golf
- Arena/stadium
- Skiing
- Sailing
- Wind surfing

- Surfing
- Canoeing/rafting
- Mineral/thermal spa
- Beach resort
- Amusement/theme park
- Casino
- Horse racing
- Waterskiing
- Seaport
- Mountain refuge/pasture
- Rambling/hiking area
- Viewpoint
- Mountain railroad
- Leisure bath

Principal travel routes

- Auto route
- Rail road
- Shipping route

Scale 1:950,000

0   10   20 Kilometers

Remarkable landscapes and natural monuments

- UNESCO World Natural Heritage
- Cave
- River landscape
- Lake country
- Nature park
- National park (landscape)
- National park (flora)
- National park (fauna)
- Biosphere reserve
- Wildlife reserve
- Protected area for sea-lions/seals
- Zoo/safari park
- Botanical garden
- Coastal landscape
- Beach
- Island

Remarkable Cities and Cultural monuments

- UNESCO World Cultural Heritage
- Romanesque church
- Gothic church
- Christian monastery
- Cultural landscape
- Historical city scape
- Castle/fortress/fort
- Palace
- Technical/industrial monument
- Remarkable lighthouse
- Remarkable bridge
- Windmill
- Striking building
- Museum
- Open-air museum
- Tourist information centre

Sport and leisure destination

- Arena/stadium
- Sailing
- Wind surfing
- Beach resort

BALTIC SEA

DENMARK
GERMANY

Møn

Falster

Rødsand

Vordingborg

Næstved

Nykøbing F

Nationalpark
Vorpommersche
Boddenlandschaft

Darß

Zingst

Barth

STRALSUND

Bergen

Sassnitz

Nationalpark
Jasmund

Rügen

Putbus

Biosphärenreservat
Südost-Rügen

Rügischer
Bodden

Greifswalder Bodden

Pomeranian Bay

Grimmen

GREIFSWALD

Wolgast

Warnemünde

Bad Doberan

ROSTOCK

Güstrow

Bützow

Damgarten

Ribnitz

Demmin

Anklam

SWINOUJSCIE

Wolin

Usedom

Teterow

Waren

Neubrandenburg

Pasewalk

Ueckermünde

Stettin Lagoon

Mecklenburgische Seenplatte

Müritz

Nationalpark
Mecklenburgische

Neustrelitz

SZCZECIN

Remarkable Cities and Cultural monuments

- ☐ UNESCO World Cultural Heritage
- ☐ Pre- and early history
- ▲ Places of Christian cultural interest
- ▲ Romanesque church
- ♦ Gothic church
- ♦ Christian monastery
- ♦ Cultural landscape
- ♦ Historical city scape
- ♜ Castle/fortress/fort
- ♜ Castle ruin
- ♟ Palace
- ⚒ Technical/industrial monument
- ♯ Windmill
- ♯ Striking building
- ♯ Museum
- ♯ Open-air museum

Sport and leisure destination

- ⚓ Arena/stadium
- ♞ Horse racing
- ⛵ Sailing
- ⛱ Beach resort

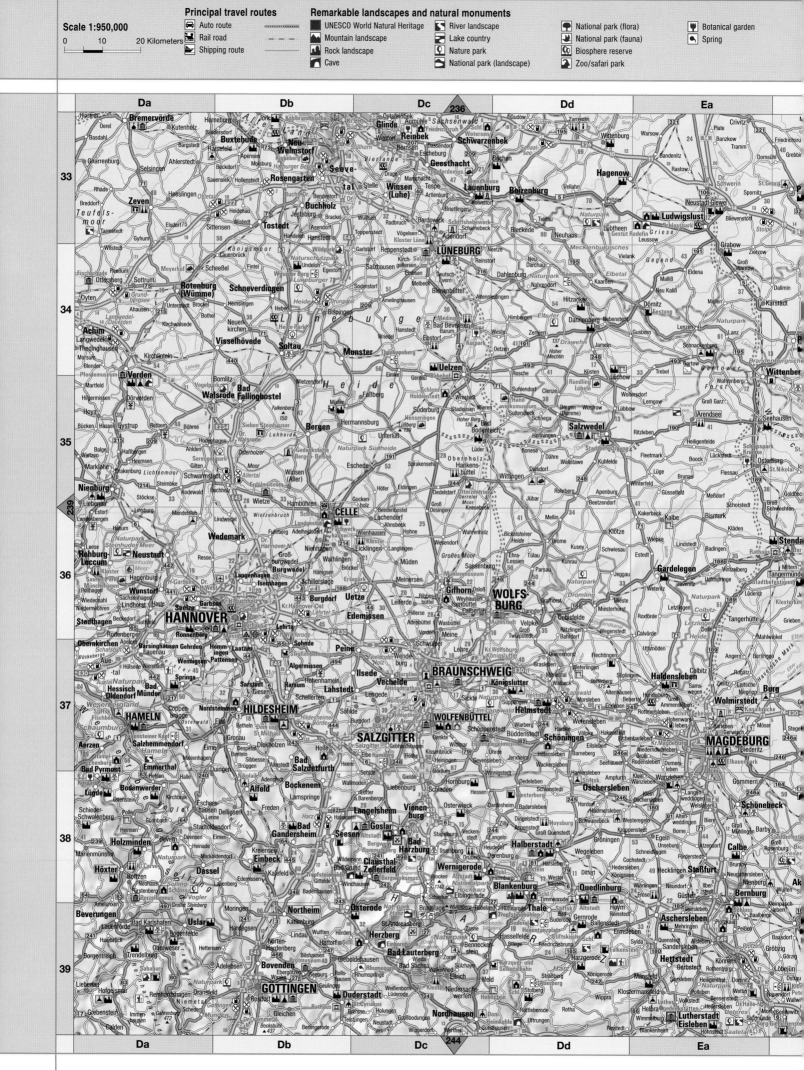

Remarkable Cities and Cultural monuments

- UNESCO World Cultural Heritage
- Pre- and early history
- Places of Christian cultural interest
- Romanesque church
- Gothic church
- Christian monastery
- Cultural landscape
- Historical city scape
- Castle/fortress/fort
- Castle ruin
- Palace
- Windmill
- Striking building
- Monument
- Museum
- Open-air museum

Sport and leisure destination

- Arena/stadium
- Horse racing
- Leisure pool
- Mineral/thermal spa

	Ec	Ed	Fa	Fb	Fc

Principal travel routes

Auto route
Rail road
Shipping route

Remarkable landscapes and natural monuments

UNESCO World Natural Heritage
Mountain landscape
Rock landscape
Extinct volcano

Cave
River landscape
Lake country
Fossil site

Nature park
National park (landscape)
National park (flora)
National park (fauna)

Biosphere reserve
Zoo/safari park
Botanical garden
Spring

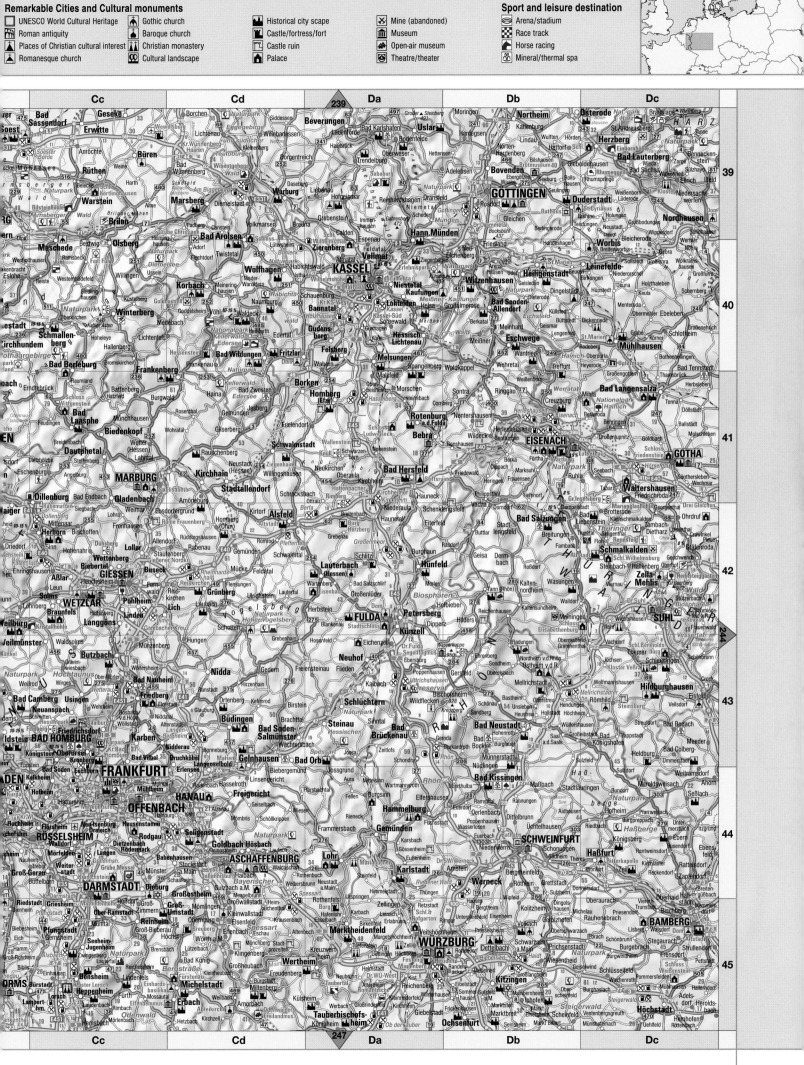

Remarkable Cities and Cultural monuments

- ☐ UNESCO World Cultural Heritage
- ☐ Roman antiquity
- ▲ Places of Christian cultural interest
- ☆ Romanesque church
- ⛪ Gothic church
- ⛪ Baroque church
- ⛪ Christian monastery
- ⛪ Cultural landscape
- ⛫ Historical city scape
- ⛨ Castle/fortress/fort
- ⛫ Castle ruin
- ⛩ Palace
- ⛏ Mine (abandoned)
- 🏛 Museum
- 🏛 Open-air museum
- 🎭 Theatre/theater

Sport and leisure destination

- 🏟 Arena/stadium
- 🏁 Race track
- 🏇 Horse racing
- ♨ Mineral/thermal spa

Principal travel routes

- Auto route
- Rail road
- Shipping route

Remarkable landscapes and natural monuments

- UNESCO World Natural Heritage
- Mountain landscape
- Rock landscape
- Ravine/canyon
- Cave
- River landscape
- Waterfall/rapids
- Lake country
- Nature park
- National park (landscape)
- National park (flora)
- National park (fauna)
- Biosphere reserve
- Wildlife reserve
- Spring

Scale 1:950,000

0   10   20 Kilometers

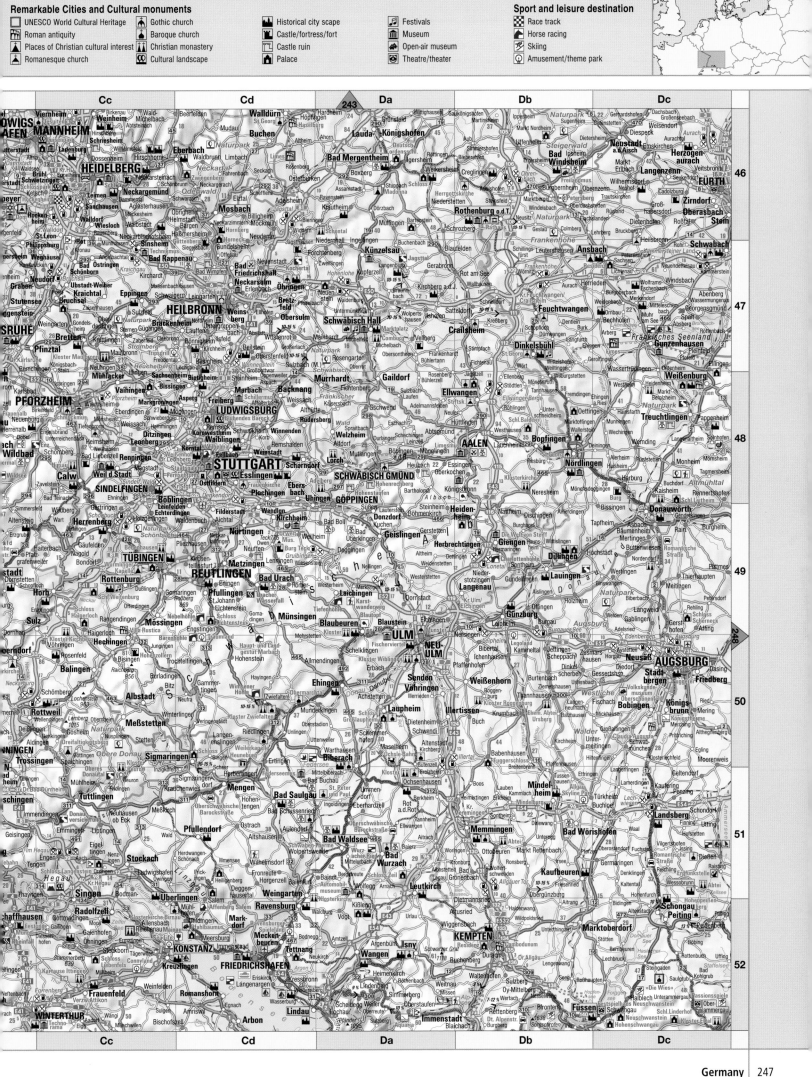

Remarkable Cities and Cultural monuments

☐ UNESCO World Cultural Heritage   ⛪ Gothic church
⛪ Roman antiquity   ⛪ Baroque church
⛪ Places of Christian cultural interest   ⛪ Christian monastery
⛪ Romanesque church   Cultural landscape

🏛 Historical city scape
🏰 Castle/fortress/fort
🏰 Castle ruin
🏰 Palace

🎵 Festivals
🏛 Museum
🏚 Open-air museum
🎭 Theatre/theater

Sport and leisure destination

🏁 Race track
🏇 Horse racing
⛷ Skiing
🎡 Amusement/theme park

Remarkable Cities and Cultural monuments

☐ UNESCO World Cultural Heritage	♖ Baroque church	♜ Castle/fortress/fort	⛪ Museum
🏛 Roman antiquity	⛪ Christian monastery	♜ Castle ruin	🏛 Open-air museum
🏛 Places of Christian cultural interest	♜ Cultural landscape	🏛 Palace	🎭 Theatre/theater
⛪ Gothic church	🏰 Historical city scape	🏭 Technical/industrial monument	🏅 Olympics

Sport and leisure destination

🏟 Arena/stadium	⛳ Golf
🏊 Mineral/thermal spa	🎡 Amusement/theme park

The entries in the index refer to the picture section and the maps. The index entry is followed, corresponding to the map entry concerned, by a symbol (explained on p. 235) which explains sights by type. They are followed by the page number for the picture section and, finally, internet addresses are given which facilitate rapid accessing of more updated information on the places of interest and the sights to see described in this book. Most entries on the picture pages are also to be found in the map section, which, moreover, provides a wealth of further important tips for visitors.

From left: historic port warehouses in Hamburg; Lübeck's Holstenhafen port on the River Trave, Frank O. Gehry's Neuer Zollhof office complex in Düsseldorf; flags at the German Mining Museum, Bochum.

From left: Wilhelma zoological-botanic gardens in Stuttgart; Mirror Hall in Herrenchiemsee Castle, Chiemgau; Oktoberfest and Nymphenburg Palace in Munich; Bertradaburg fortress at Mürlenbach, Eifel.

From left: Western shore of Darss-Zingst peninsula on the Baltic Sea; Museumsufer in Frankfurt; Potsdamer Platz, Berlin; Wörlitz Castle in Dessau-Wörlitz Gardens; the legendary Wartburg at Eisenach.

Photo credits

Abbreviations:
B = Bieker
C = Corbis
Hub = Bildagentur Huber
IFA = IFA Bilderteam
Mau = Mauritius
P = Premium
W = Wandmacher
Z = Zielske

Numbering from top left to bottom right.

Cover: front: Zielske
Titel B, 2/3 Z, 4/5 B, 6/7 Z, 7.1 P/Sekai Bun-ka, 7.2 Hub, 7.3 P/C&R Dörr, 7.4 Böttcher, 7.5 Z, 7.6 Getty, 7.7 Z, 7.8 IFA/Vahl, 7.9 B, 7.10 B, 7.11 P/Waldkirch, 8/9 P/Sekai Bun-ka, 8.1 laif/Lange, 10/11 P/Milse, 10.1 Hub, 10.2-4 P/delphoto, 12/13 Z, 12.1 laif/Specht, 12.2 Z, 14/15 Z, 14.1 laif/Selbach, 14.2 laif/A.Hub, 14.3,4 B, 14.5,6 laif/A.Hub, 14.7 B, 14.8 laif/Selbach, 16/17 laif/Selbach, 16.1 IFA/Aberkam, 16.2,3 laif/Kohlbecher, 16.4 P, 16.5 König, 16.6 P, 16.7 König, 18/19 Z, 18.1 P, 18.2 Hub, 18.3 Z, 18.4 laif/Kirchner, 18.5 Hub, 20/21 Z, 20.1 P/Wothe, 20.2,3 laif/Modrow, 21.1 Hub, 21.2 Z, 21.3 Freyer, 22/23 Z, 22.1 laif/Ebert, 22.2 laif/Modrow, 22.3 laif/Multhaupt, 22.4-6 Z, 24/25 und 24.1 Z, 24.2,3 W, 24.4,5 laif/ Modrow, 24.6 W, 25.1-3 W, 26/27 Hub, 26.1 B, 28/29 laif/ Hahn, 28.1 B, 28.2 W, 29.1 B, 29.2 Hub, 30/31 Z, 30.1 laif/Zuder, 30.2 laif/Tjaden, 30.3 Z, 32/33 P/Jorens-Beldé, 32.1,2 Z, 32.3 laif/ A.Hub, 32.4 W, 32.5 Schilgen, 32.6 W, 33.1 Z, 33.2,3 W, 34/35 und 34.1 Hub, 34.2 C/Adam Woolfitt, 34.3 Mohnheim/Jochen Helle, 34.4,5 C/Adam Woolfit, 34.6 W, 36/37 Klammet, 36.1 akg/ images, 36.2,3 Freyer, 37.1 Hub/Gräfenhain/Damm, 37.2 B, 37.3 Klammet, 38/39 und 38.1 W, 38.2 DFA/Babovic, 38.3,4 W, 40/41 Alamy/© Stockmaritime, Trademark of GentCom GmbH, 40.1 laif/Kirchner, 42/43 f1 online/ Steiner, 42.1,2 laif/ Kirchner, 43.1 Böttcher, 43.2 Hub, 43.3 DFA, 44/45 Z, 46/47 D.C. Zahn, 46.1 P/C&R Dörr, 46.2 laif/Aberkam, 46.3 P/C&R Dörr, 48/49 P/C&R Dörr, 48.1-49.2 Z, 50/51 laif/Adenis/GAFF, 50.1 laif/ Modrow, 50.2-6 Z, 52/53 Z, 52.1 Böttcher, 53.1,2 laif/Kirchner, 53.3,4 P/C&R Dörr, 53.5 laif/Kirchner, 54/55 laif/ Kirchner,

54.1,2 Hub, 54.3 N.N., 54.4/55.1 Hub, 55.2 Böttcher, 55.3 N.N., 55.4 laif/Babovic, 56/57 Böttcher, 56.1 P/Panoramic Images, 58/59 und 58.1 laif/Zahn, 58.2 Z, 58.3 Hub, 58.4,5 Böttcher, 60/61 laif/Maecke/GAFF, 60.1 laif/Boening/Zenit, 60.2 Schilgen, 62/63 Huber, 62.1 laif/Adenis/GAFF, 62.2 laif/Langrock/Zenit, 64/65 laif/Boening, 64.1,2 Böttcher, 64.3 Mau, 64.4 laif/Galli, 64.5 Schilgen, 65.1 Böttcher, 65.2 laif/Boe-ning, 65.3,4 laif/Galli, 66/67 laif/Zahn, 66.1 Böttcher, 67.1,2 Freyer, 68/69 laif/Boening/ Zenit, 70/71 Böttcher, 70.1,2 DFA/Scheib-ner, 70.3 Z, 70.4 DFA/ Scheibner, 72/73 Z, 72.1 P/Sixty-Six, 74/75 Z, 74.1-3 B, 74.4 DFA, 76/77 B, 76.1-3 Romeis, 77.1-5 B, 78/79 DFA, 78.1 Klaes, 78.2 B, 79.1 Z. 79.2 laif/Wieland, 79.3 laif/A.Hub, 79.4 laif/Per-kovic, 80/81 und 80.1,2 B, 80.3 laif/A.Hub, 80.4 IFA/Schlösser, 81.1 Z, 81.2 B, 81.3 Z, 81.4 DFA/Vollmer, 82/83 Z, 82.1 W, 82.2-83.2 B, 84/85 laif/Klein, 84.1 laif/Linke, 84.2 laif/Orgando, 84.3/85.1 laif/Linke, 86/87 laif/G.Huber, 86.1,2 Dietrich, 87.1 laif/G. Huber, 87.2 laif/Orgando, 87.3 laif/Linke, 88/89 Z, 88.1 Hub, 88.2 DFA, 88.3 Hub, 88.4 laif, 88.5 laif/G.Huber, 89.1 C/Ali Mey-er, 90/91 IFA/Ostgathe, 90.1 Z, 90.2 Klam-met, 90.3 Florian Mohnheim, 91.1,2 laif/ Gaasterland, 92/93 B, 92.1 Z, 92.2-4 B, 92.5,6 laif/Kreuels, 92.7 B, 94/95 Getty, 94.1 IFA/Panstock, 96/97 IFA/Lecom, 96.1 IFA/Gich, 96.2 Hub/Klaes, 96.3,4 Hub/R. Schmid, 98/99 C/Reuters, 98.1 C/Tom Szlu-kovenyi, 98.2-4 C/Reuters, 100/101 Hub, 100.1 Mohnheim, 101.1 IFA, 101.2 Hub, 101.3 IFA, 101.4 P/Orion Press, 102/103 und 102.1 laif/Heuer, 102.2 laif/Eisenmann, 102.3 laif/Linke, 102.4 Hub, 102.5 P/Schulz-ki, 104/105 Mau, 104.1 Hub, 104.2 Z, 104.3 Hub/Gräfenhain, 104.4 laif/Gaasterland, 104.5 B, 106/107 Hub/ Schmid/Radelt, 106.1-3 Hub, 108/109 Z, 108.1 König, 108.2 B, 108.3 P, 109.1 laif/Kreuels, 109.2 laif, 110/111 Z, 112/113 laif/Emmler 112.1-3 laif/Meyer, 112.4,5 laif/Emmler, 114/115 Z, 114.1-3 Herzig, 115.1 laif/Emmler, 115.2 Z, 116/117 Wackenhut, 116.1 N.N., 116.2 laif/Modrow, 116.3 Schilgen, 116.4 laif/ Modrow, 118/119 Z, 118.1 laif/Emmler, 118.2 Schilgen, 118.3,4 laif/Emmler, 118.5 Z, 118.6 Klaes, 120/121 Mau/Raimund Lin-ke, 120.1-121.2 laif/Emmler, 122/123 Z, 122.1 Mau, 122.2 Herzig, 122.3 IFA/Everts,

122.4 Herzig, 124/125 und 124.1 Z, 124.2 C/James L. Amos, 124.3,4 photo digital GmbH, 126/127 Z, 126.1 C/James L. Amos, 128/129 laif/Babovic, 128.1 Z, 129.1 (small) emo-pictures, 129.2 (large) laif/Westrich, 130/131 laif/Zanettini, 130.1 laif/Babovic, 130.2-131.4 laif/Babovic, 132/133 IFA/Sie-bert, 132.1,2 photo digital GmbH, 132.3 Dietrich, 132.4 W, 134/135 IFA/Vahl, 134.1 IFA/Harris, 136/137 Z, 136.1 Hub, 136.2 DFA, 137.1 Herzig, 137.2 Z, 138/139 und 138.1 Romeis, 138.2 Z, 138.3 Hub, 140/141 und 140.1-4 Z, 140.5 laif/ Kreuels, 142/143 Z, 142.1 DFA/Babovic, 142.2 laif/Modrow, 142.3 DFA/Babovic, 142.4 laif/Modrow, 142.5 Z, 142.6 Mohnheim, 144/145 Z, 144.1 P/Hänel, 145.1 Z, 145.2 IFA/Fischer, 145.3 Z, 146/147 laif/ Hahn, 146.1-3 Her-zig, 148/149 und 148.1,2 Z, 149.1 laif/ Granser, 149.2 laif/Huber, 150/151 Z, 150.1 Staatl. Kunstsammlungen Dresden/bridge-manart.com, 150.2 Z, 152/153 und 152.1 laif/Kirchner, 152.2,3 laif/Jehnichen, 153.1 laif/ Kirchner, 153.2 laif/Huber, 154/155 und 154.1 Z, 154.2 laif/Maecke/GAFF, 154.3/ 155.1 Z, 156/157 und 156.1 Z, 157.1-4 Hub, 158/159 laif/Gaasterland, 158.1 Hub, 158.2 Fnoxx/ Arnulf Hettrich, 159.1 atur/ Halbe/Roland, 159.2,3 transit/Thomas Hae-rtrich, 160/161 B, 160.1 Romeis, 162/163 Romeis, 162.1 B, 162.2 Romeis, 163.1 Z, 163.2,3 Romeis, 164/165 B, 164.1 P/D. Esor, 164.2 laif/Mueller, 164.3 Hub, 164.4 Herzig, 164.5 Romeis, 164.6 Mau, 166/167 C/Her-bert Kehrer, 166.1 Schilgen, 167.1 GRAFFI-TI/Joachim E. Roettgers, 167.2 laif/Müller, 167.3 P/Otto, 168/169 laif/Emmler, 168.1,2 B, 168.3 laif/Galli, 170/171 laif/Gonzalez, 170.1-4 B, 171.1 laif/Bungert, 172/173 Hub/R. Schmid, 172.1-3 B, 174/175 Hub, 174.1-3 laif/Eid, 175.1 B, 175.2 laif/Eiser-mann, 175.3 Hub, 175.4 laif/Eisermann, 175.5 laif/Raach, 175.6,7 Romeis, 176/177 Hub, 176.1,2 B, 177.1 Romeis, 177.2 Die-trich, 177.3 Mau, 177.4 Hub, 178/179 Ro-meis, 178.1, 2 P, 178.3 C/Roger Wilms-hurst/Frantz Lane, 179.1 Z, 179.2 IFA/Stad-ler, 179.3 Hub, 179.4 B, 180/181 Freyer, 180.1 B, 181.1 Freyer, 181.2 C/Vanni Archi-ve, 181.3 Freyer, 182/183 Z, 182.1-183.3 B, 184/185 laif/Emmler, 184.1 B, 184.2 laif/ Emmler, 184.3/185.1 laif/Emmler, 185.2 Z, 185.3 laif/Emmler, 185.4 Z, 186/187 B, 186.1 Hub, 186.2 laif/Heuer, 186.3 Kustos,

186.4,5 B, 188/189 B, 188.1 Z, 190/191 Hub, 190.1 Z, 190.2 IFA/Rauch, 191.1 Klam-met, 191.2 IFA/Photo digital, 192/193 Rom-eis, 192.1 C/Jim Zuckermann, 193.1 laif/Hu-ber, 194/195 B, 194.1 Z, 195.1 Wackenhut, 195.2 Hub, 195.3 Romeis, 195.4 Z, 195.5 Wackenhut, 195.6 laif/Kirchgessner, 196/197 Z, 196.1 Freyer, 197.1 C/Elizabeth Opalenik, 198/199 Z, 198.1 Hub, 198.2 Wackenhut, 198.3 C/Arthur Thévenart, 198.4 Hub, 200/201 laif/Bialobrzeski, 200.1 C/Jon Hicks, 200.2,3 Z, 202/203 P/Panora-mic Images/T.Winz, 202.1 Romeis, 202.2 Hub, 202.3 Freyer, 202.4 Hub, 202.5 Klam-met, 204/205 P/Panoramic Images/T. Winz, 204.1,2 B, 204.3 Freyer, 204.4 B, 204.5 Z, 204.6 B, 206/207 Z, 206.1 Hub, 206.2 Schil-gen, 206.3 Hub, 206.4 Z, 208/209 Mau, 208.1 Hub, 208.2 Mau/image broker/Bahn-mueller, 210/211 Z, 210.1 IFA/Wittek, 211.1 Mau, 211.2 Delphoto, 211.3 IFA/Schulz, 211.4,5 Hub, 212/213 laif/A.Hub, 212.1 IFA/Lecom, 212.2 B, 214/215 DFA, 214.1 At-tantide/Schapowalow, 214.2 Klammet/Ra-delt, 214.3 Hub, 216/217 Z, 216.1 laif/A. Hub, 216.2 Romeis, 216.3 Bildagentur-onli-ne/A. Forkel, 217.1 laif/A.Hub, 217.2 C/ Adam Woolfitt, 218/219 IFA/Helweg, 218.1-3 Romeis, 219.1 IFA/Jon Arnold Images, 219.2 Romeis, 219.3 IFA/Siebig, 220/221 Romeis, 220.1 Franz Marc Frei, 220.2 P/ Buss, 220.3 laif/ Adenis/GAFF, 220.4 laif/ Henglein/ Klover, 220.5-7 Franz Marc Frei, 222/223 Franz Marc Frei, 222.1 Romeis, 222.2 IFA/Shashin Koubou, 222.3 laif/ Adenis/GAFF, 222.4 laif/Back, 223.1 laif/ Adenis/GAFF, 223.2 IFA/Steinberger, 224/225 Dr. C. Zahn, 224.1 LOOK GmbH/ Florian Werner, 225.1 LOOK/ Heinz Wohner, 225.2 Arco Digital Image/ Harting, 225.3 C/Ray Juno, 226/227 Z, 226.1 Mau, 226.2 P, 226.3-5 B, 226.6 Romeis, 228/229 IFA/Stad-ler, 230/231 Bernd Ritschel, 230.1 IFA/Pho-to Digital, 231.1 IFA/F. Schmidt, 231.2 Mau/ Westend61, 231.3 C/F. Damm/Zefa, 232/233 P/Waldkirch, 234/235 C/Michaela Rehle, 250.1,2 Z, 251.1 P/Sixty-Six, 251.2 B, 252.1 P/Panoramic Images/T.Winz, 252.2 IFA/Stadler, 252.3 IFA/Steinberger, 253.1 IFA/Helweg, 253.2 Hub/Klaes, 254.1 P/C&R Dörr, 254.2 laif/Emmler, 254.3 laif/Adenis/ GAFF, 255.1 Romeis, 255.2 Z

MONACO BOOKS is an imprint of Verlag Wolfgang Kunth

© Verlag Wolfgang Kunth GmbH & Co.KG, Munich, 2009
Concept: Wolfgang Kunth
Editing and design: Verlag Wolfgang Kunth GmbH&Co.KG

For distribution please contact:

Monaco Books
c/o Verlag Wolfgang Kunth, Königinstr.11
80539 München, Germany
Tel: +49 / 89/45 80 20 23
Fax: +49 / 89/ 45 80 20 21
info@kunth-verlag.de

www.monacobooks.com
www.kunth-verlag.de

Text: Norbert Lewandowski, Eckhard Schuster, Walter M. Weiss
Translation: Alison Moffat-McLynn

The information and facts presented in the book have been extensively researched and edited for accuracy. The publishers, authors, and editors, cannot, however, guarantee that all of the information in the book is entirely accurate or up to date at the time of publi-cation. The publishers are grateful for any suggestions or corrections that would improve the content of this work.

The Adventure Guide

Written by Catherine Saunders

Contents

NOW FOR BREAKING NEWS FROM OLIVIA AT AMBERSANDS BEACH!

Andrea

Emma

Stephanie

Mia

Olivia

4

Introduction

Friendship ✿ Individuality ✿ Teamwork ✿ Adventure

Andrea, Emma, Stephanie, Mia, and Olivia are the best of friends. They are always there for each other, no matter what. Each girl has her own individual talents, interests, and dreams for the future, but when the five of them get together something special always happens!

Together, the girls can achieve anything they want to. Whether it is helping others, learning something new, or just throwing the most amazing parties, they can do it. They know when to work hard and when to relax, when to be serious and when to have fun. For Andrea, Emma, Stephanie, Mia, and Olivia, life is an amazing adventure. But above all, the girls know what's truly important—being a good friend.

**Come and join the LEGO® Friends
in and around Heartlake City...**

Welcome to Heartlake City

Beautiful Heartlake City takes its name from the stunning heart-shaped lake that it is built around. Its friendly residents think that it is the best place to live, and it is always bustling with fabulous things to see and do.

Andrea's House

Clearspring Falls

Mia's Magic Stage

Stables

Sunshine Ranch

Surrounded by acres of gorgeous countryside, Sunshine Ranch is a busy working farm. It supplies a lot of the city's fruit and vegetables and is home to hundreds of animals.

Heartlake Vet

Animals are welcome in Heartlake City. Injured creatures are cared for at the Heartlake Vet by Dr. Sophie, or across town at the new clinic.

Heartlake Shopping Mall

On the outskirts of the city, the Heartlake Shopping Mall is the place for fashion, food, and hanging out with friends.

Emma's House

Emma's house is one of the newest houses in town. It was designed by her mother.

Beach House

Ambersands Beach is a great spot for watersports. Stephanie is lucky enough to have a beach house there.

Olivia's House

Olivia's house is typical of the pretty, modern style found all around Heartlake City. Visitors are always guaranteed a friendly welcome!

The Lighthouse

One of Heartlake City's most famous landmarks, the lighthouse is a great place to explore. Learn about its history, then grab a tasty ice cream.

Butterfly Beauty Shop

Pet Salon

Hair Salon

Heartlake High

City Park Café

City Pool

Ambersands Beach

Which friend are you?

Heartlake City is home to five best friends with very different personalities. Mia, Olivia, Stephanie, Emma, and Andrea complement each other and each one has something important to teach the others.

Start

Do you love being the center of attention?

YES
I love to stand out from the crowd!

NO
I'm more of a team player.

Do you prefer animals to technology?

Are you the most organized person in your group?

YES
I always have everything under control.

NO
Sometimes, I can be a little scatty.

Do you prefer giving makeovers to putting on shows?

YES
I always know what looks good on my friends!

8

You're Mia

Mia is a caring and loving person. She adores animals, but will do anything for her friends, too. Mia is a calm and kind friend.

You're Olivia

Olivia loves science and technology. She can be a little shy at parties, but she is a hard-working and practical friend.

YES

I love all things furry, fishy or feathered.

You're Stephanie

Stephanie is organized, sociable, and energetic. Sometimes people find it hard to keep up with her, but she is a popular and helpful friend.

NO

I'm a super science fan and tech wizard.

You're Emma

Emma is a creative and talented person. She wants to make the world a more beautiful place. Emma is a positive and loyal friend.

You're Andrea

Andrea is ambitious and confident. She is determined to be a singing star. Andrea is a fun, sociable, and interesting friend.

NO

I'm a natural performer and love to sing in public.

Olivia

I think Heartlake City is the greatest place in the world. My family moved here a while back and I've made some amazing friends. I can do so many wonderful things here, from hiking in Whispering Woods, to surfing at Ambersands Beach. My life is never boring!

LET'S COOK DINNER ON THE BARBECUE TONIGHT!

Mom and Dad

My parents are busy people, but they always try to make time for me. Mom is a doctor and Dad is Editor-in-Chief at the NewsRoom. I'm really proud of them both.

My style is casual, practical, and relaxed. Long shorts are perfect for surfing!

My Top 3 Inventions

Zobo—a remote-controlled robot. He's cute and very smart.

My own app—it controls the lighting and orders room service at the Heartlake hotel.

A special carriage—for horse-drawn tours of the city.

My pets

I have two super-cute pets. Kitty is a nine-year-old house cat who loves to find a sunny spot to nap in. Scarlett is just a puppy. My aunt Sophie, the Heartlake vet, gave her to me.

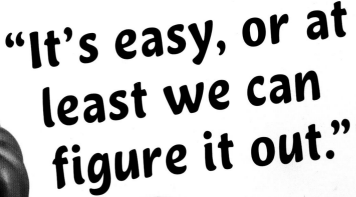

"It's easy, or at least we can figure it out."

Special place

My favorite subjects are science and math and I love finding out how things work. I spend a lot of time in my workshop, building things and inventing new gadgets.

This surfboard was a present from my grandparents. At first I was a nervous surfer, but now I love it!

IT'S TIME TO HIT THE WAVES!

My wheels

Most mornings, I load my surfboard onto my beach buggy and head off to the ocean. I've made a few small changes to the buggy, such as heated seats. That's what inventors do!

11

Olivia's inventions

Olivia loves to find out how things work. Then she thinks about how she can make them even better! Olivia is passionate about science and wants to use her skills to make life easier and more fun for the people she loves.

Tree house

When Olivia found an old tree house in her back garden, she saw its potential immediately. She drew up some plans, fixed it up and now her friends have a cool place to hang out.

Fruit stall

Olivia loves visiting Mia's grandparents at Sunshine Ranch—they are so kind. Olivia wanted to find a way to help them, so she built this farm stall. Now they can sell their fresh produce.

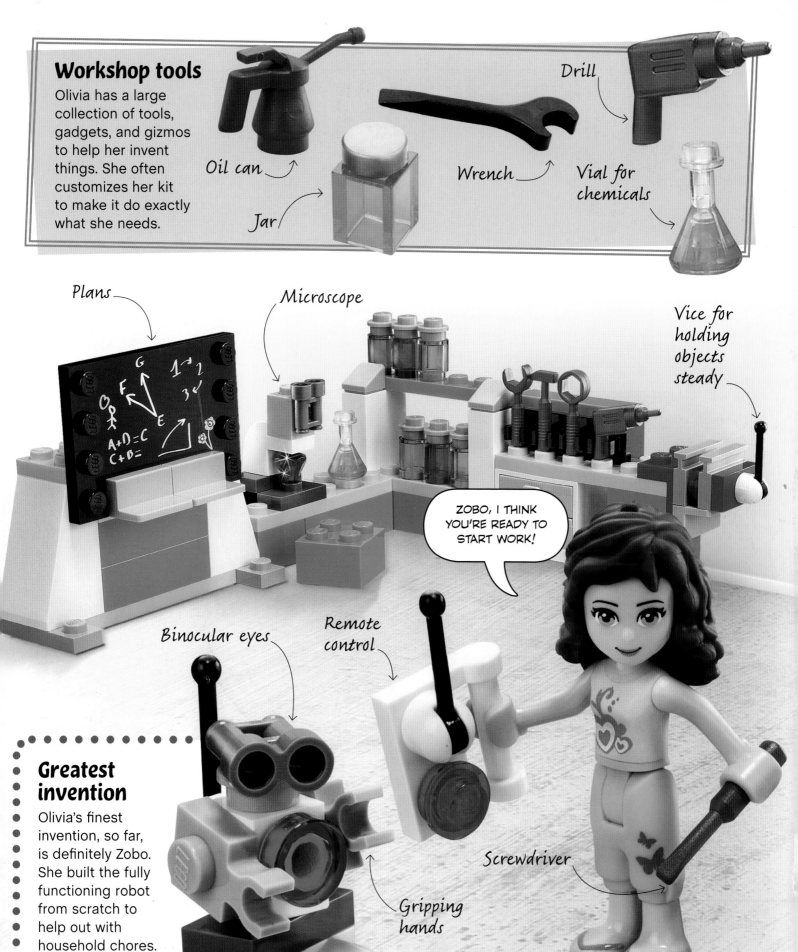

Workshop tools

Olivia has a large collection of tools, gadgets, and gizmos to help her invent things. She often customizes her kit to make it do exactly what she needs.

Oil can

Jar

Drill

Wrench

Vial for chemicals

Plans

Microscope

Vice for holding objects steady

ZOBO, I THINK YOU'RE READY TO START WORK!

Binocular eyes

Remote control

Greatest invention

Olivia's finest invention, so far, is definitely Zobo. She built the fully functioning robot from scratch to help out with household chores.

Gripping hands

Screwdriver

13

Emma

I'm inspired by everything in Heartlake City, from the beautiful scenery to my amazing friends. I love to paint, sketch, design, photograph, and create. I see beauty and new ideas everywhere. My friends say I'm a dreamer, but I say that dreams can come true if you try hard enough!

> THIS KITCHEN IS GORGEOUS. WELL DONE, MOM AND DAD!

New home

My family have just moved into a new house. It's extra-special because my mom, who's an architect, designed it and my interior designer dad decorated it. I love it!

Fashion should be bold, brave, and fun. This cute jacket says "serious news reporter".

Perfect pets

I like to look fabulous and so does my poodle, Lady. I also have an elegant horse named Robin, and a cute cat named Jewel.

My Top 3 Projects

Heartlake High TV—students need to know what's going on.

Heartlake Hair—Natasha and I have some amazing ideas.

Emma's Design Show—my new internet craft series.

"That's SO you!"

I talk into this microphone to deliver my Heartlake News reports. Now, back to the studio!

DON'T MOVE A FEATHER, KIKI. I'VE NEARLY FINISHED.

Being creative

I love experimenting with color, whether it is through my clothes, my hair or my art. Kiki the parrot is the most amazing shade of green. I want to get it just right.

SWIM BETWEEN THE FLAGS, PLEASE!

On duty

I love swimming, so a summer job as a lifeguard at the beach is perfect for me. I'm responsible for keeping the kids safe. It's a tough job, but when my shift ends, I have a relaxing swim.

Emma's inspiration

Emma is buzzing with new ideas. Everything around her inspires her—from the color of the water in Lake Heart, to the texture of a leaf in Whispering Woods. Emma always aims to create something fabulous.

> THIS FABRIC WOULD MAKE A CUTE SKIRT FOR STEPHANIE.

Hot or not?

When Emma wants to find out about the latest beauty trends, she heads to the **Butterfly Beauty Shop** to see her friend Sarah. Emma values her expert opinion—beautician **Sarah** always knows exactly what's hot and what's definitely not.

Design studio

Emma has her own **studio** where she can work on her design ideas. It is a bright, clean, **creative space** with everything she needs—her laptop, her mood board, her sketchbook, her sewing kit, and rolls of fabric. No one else is allowed in here!

I THINK IT'S TIME TO CHANGE YOUR LOOK, EMMA!

I LOVE IT! I FEEL LIKE A DIFFERENT PERSON.

Style tip

Emma doesn't stick to fashion rules—she breaks them! Her golden rule is that if you feel good, you look good. Just be confident!

Experimenting

Emma enjoys designing her own clothes, but she loves shopping too. She likes to go to the **Heartlake Shopping Mall** and try on hundreds of outfits. Emma is planning a **new party look** with Stephanie's help. She's going to call it "snow princess."

Changing style

Emma likes to change her look frequently. She prefers to start fashions, rather than follow them. When Natasha suggests a **radical new haircut**, Emma doesn't hesitate. She encourages her friends to make **bold fashion choices**, too.

Mia

I'm happiest when I'm outside. Heartlake City is full of amazing places to see and I never know where my next adventure might take me. My big passion is animals. In fact, my friends often joke that I prefer animals to people. Well, maybe sometimes...

> FIRST, LET'S BRUSH YOUR SILKY COAT, SCARLETT.

Puppy training

I've trained my puppy, Charlie, to fetch and sit when I tell him to. He's so good, that Olivia has asked me to train her puppy, Scarlett, too. I can't wait!

My Top 3 Ways to relax

Grooming Bella—I tell her my problems. She understands!

Playing the drums—it's loud, fast, and I love it!

Nature documentaries—animals are just fascinating.

Work experience

I'm pretty sure that my career will involve working with animals. I often help the local vet, Dr. Sophie. I might become a vet like her, or an animal psychologist.

> *Skateboarding is a cool sport, but it's all about balance. I think I have it!*

"Let's get to work!"

My big adventure
On a rescue mission in the jungle I got to fly a helicopter to save an animal in trouble. It was thrilling but scary!

My mom loves ice cream, so I'm delivering this mango one via skateboard!

Special friend
I've had my horse, Bella, since she was a foal. We often explore Whispering Woods together or enter jumping competitions. She's a good listener, too.

Bella

How to train a puppy

Mia loves caring for animals, but it can be hard work! Animals need discipline, as well as lots of love. Follow Mia's expert advice to find out how to turn cute but naughty puppies into obedient, adorable show champions.

1 Practice

Puppies like Max need to do things lots of times in order to remember. Every skill, obstacle or command must be practiced several times a day.

Practice jump

Charlie's kennel

2 Rest

It's important not to overwork puppies. They're only young, so they need plenty of rest time. Make sure their kennels are clean and comfortable, too.

Bone

3 Treats

Rewarding puppies when they do something right is a great way to help them learn. Bones and dog biscuits are puppies' favorite snacks.

COME ON SCARLETT, YOU CAN DO IT!

Scarlett

Be positive

Mia's voice is an important part of puppy training. She keeps her commands simple so the puppies can understand and always says "good girl" when her puppy does well.

Seesaw

Trophy

Having fun

After a few weeks of training, Mia likes to enter her puppies into dog shows. The puppies always have fun and it's a great way to see if her training has worked!

21

Andrea

For me, life isn't a dress rehearsal, it's one big show! I love to sing, dance, and act whenever I can. My dream is to become a professional performer and I'm determined to succeed. My friends are my biggest fans—they always sit in the front row, cheering me on.

> THIS IS A NEW SONG, DEDICATED TO MY FRIENDS.

> *An ice-cold juice is perfect for relaxing when I'm not performing.*

Practice

I practice singing every day. It's important to make sure my voice is strong. I also compose all my own songs and dance routines.

My special pet

Jazz is the first pet I've ever owned and I adore him. I chose him because he is full of energy, just like me. Jazz's two favorite hobbies are eating carrots and listening to me sing.

"Music puts life in full color"

Staying healthy

Performers can't afford to get sick, so I like to eat healthily. The vitamin-packed super smoothies at the Heartlake Juice Bar are my favorite.

My Top 3 Dream jobs

Pop star—I'd like to top the charts with one of my songs.

Teacher—training kids how to sing and dance would be fun.

Movie actress—it would be awesome to star in a film.

Networking

I have friends all over the world, thanks to my blog, "Andrea's Alley." I write about whatever interests me and share my music.

I work hard so I love chilling out at a beach party—sun, sea, sand, and music!

WHAT SHALL I WRITE ABOUT TODAY?

How does Andrea juggle everything?

Andrea's life is never boring! From practicing to performing, waitressing to working out, she is always busy doing something interesting. But how does she fit everything into her busy life? That's easy—Andrea always has a plan.

Heartlake Café

On Monday evenings and Saturday afternoons, Andrea waits tables at the City Park Café. It's hard work, but Andrea enjoys it. She especially likes chatting to the customers.

Marie gives the Café staff free meals. After a long shift, Andrea is always very hungry!

Bedroom rehearsals

Andrea can always find time to practice singing. In free moments she sings everywhere—in the shower, while she's styling her hair, on the bus to school, and even to her pet rabbit, Jazz.

Social life

Somehow, Andrea also manages to fit in a lively and active social life. She plays soccer for her school team, and she always makes time for her friends.

Show time!

Andrea thinks that the best way to prepare herself for her future pop career is to perform in front of an audience. So, she regularly puts on evening shows for her friends and family.

Second job

In the summer, Andrea serves food and drinks at the City Pool snack bar. Her friend Isabella often stops by for a chat, and to enjoy one of Andrea's delicious strawberry smoothies.

YOU'VE GOT TO BELIEVE IN YOURSELF AND WORK HARD FOR YOUR DREAMS!

Stephanie

I love a challenge! Whether it's planning a party, starting my own business, or running a pizzeria, I just can't wait to get started. I'm super-organized and full of ideas. I love helping people in any way I can, especially my friends.

LET'S TRY A NEW FLAVOR—TRIPLE CHOCOLATE FUDGE!

Olivia made a gadget to hold my bag in place on my bike. It's awesome!

Sweet idea

I adore baking cupcakes and I had the clever idea to turn my hobby into a business. Now I run Heartlake City's premier cupcake delivery service.

Traveling in style!

I'm always very busy, so I write a daily "to-do" list. To get things done efficiently, I often run errands in my car. My neighbor's dog, Coco, usually comes along, too.

"It's all under control... almost!"

I THINK I CAN SEE HEARTLAKE HIGH WAY DOWN THERE!

Sky high

When I decide to do something, I go for it! Learning to fly planes at Heartlake Flying Club was hard work, and pretty scary, but now I can fly anywhere anytime I like.

I ride my bike to school every day. It's important to be fit and healthy.

First place

When I enter a contest, I want to win it. I'm competitive, but I always play fair. I also love winning in a team—working together makes victory even sweeter.

My Top 3 Tips for success

Plan—being organized saves time and avoids stress.

People matter—remember birthdays and important events.

Make "me" time—I relax by writing or playing my guitar.

How to run a Pizzeria

The owner of Heartlake City's Pizzeria is taking a break and she's asked Stephanie to run it for her while she's away. Stephanie may be a cupcake queen, but she doesn't know anything about pizza. How will she manage? With hard work and a little ingenuity!

1 Take the order
The Pizzeria offers fine dining at the restaurant and a gourmet takeaway service. It's a busy place!

Helmet

Pizza oven

Delivery scooter

2 Cook to perfection
Stephanie cooks all the pizzas in the huge wood-fired oven. Timing is very important— no one wants burned pizza!

3 Speedy service
Whether it's a restaurant meal or takeaway service, it's important that hungry customers get their pizzas as quickly as possible. Time is money!

The restaurant's outdoor seating area has a cozy atmosphere.

RUNNING A PIZZERIA IS HARDER THAN I THOUGHT!

Pizza paddle

Big ideas

Stephanie likes to add her own twist to things, so she's invented some new flavors, such as caramel and blueberry pizza. They haven't all been successful!

Playful pets

Whether it has feathers or fur, four legs or two, Olivia, Stephanie, Mia, Emma, and Andrea love every type of animal. Come and meet some of their favorites!

Goldie

Goldie is Olivia's pet bird, but she shares a **passion for flying** with Stephanie. Goldie and Stephanie are both members of the **Heartlake Flying Club!**

Slide

Board shorts

Tasty treats

The girls try to make sure their pets eat healthy diets, but they all deserve a treat sometimes. Jazz and Bella love carrots, whereas Lady prefers a juicy bone.

Bubbles

Olivia first met this cute turtle when she was surfing at **Ambersands Beach**. She built him his own tiki hut, with a special ramp for him to climb up and down. He loves it!

30

Yellow feathers

Bella

Mia first met Bella when she was a **foal**. Mia is devoted to her horse and **rides her every day**. Bella can't talk, but they understand each other perfectly.

Maxie the cat

Grooming brush

Lady

Emma and her **poodle**, Lady, have so much in common: they both like to look perfect at all times and have great fashion sense. They even like to **co-ordinate their outfits**!

Scissors

Hutch

Jazz

Bunny Jazz is Andrea's **first ever pet**. She is a very caring owner and always makes sure that his hutch is clean. Jazz loves it when Andrea sings to him. He's her **fluffiest fan**!

Bucket

A day in the life of
Dr. Sophie

Medical cap →

I've always loved animals, ever since I was a little girl. The only career I've ever considered is being a vet, so I can truly say I have my dream job. I'm so lucky—I get to spend every day caring for all kinds animals from bunnies to birds, horses to hedgehogs. Working at Heartlake Vet is tough, but I love it!

Green uniform

> YOU'RE PRICKLY, BUT CUTE. I'M GOING TO CALL YOU OSCAR!

Rescue animals
When the kind people of Heartlake City find a sick or abandoned animal, they bring it to me. This baby hedgehog has lost its parents, so I'm going to care for him. I'm feeding him a special formula and when he's old enough, I'll release him back into the wild.

Doing my rounds

Some sick animals have to stay in overnight. I check on them every hour to make sure they are getting better and have enough to eat and drink.

> BELLA IS MUCH BETTER. SHE'S NEARLY READY TO GO HOME, MIA.

Adorable patient

I can't help falling in love with some of my patients. This orphaned puppy, Scarlett, is so cute that I'm going to give her to my niece, Olivia. She'd love to have a puppy to train.

> YOU'RE VERY HEALTHY, SCARLETT.

Spotless, white shoes

Busy day

There's no such thing as a quiet day when you're the only vet in town. From the moment I arrive in the morning to the time the surgery closes, the phone is always ringing. I try to see every animal who needs me, no matter what time of day or night. It's not just my job, it's my passion.

33

Bunny surprise!

Stephanie adopted Daisy after finding her on a Pet Patrol. However, Stephanie didn't know that Daisy was about to become a mom! Now Stephanie has two cute baby bunnies to look after.

1 Stephanie discovers the baby bunnies when she goes to feed Daisy one morning. She is surprised, but delighted. They're so cute and cuddly!

I'M SO PROUD OF YOU DAISY. YOU'LL BE A GREAT MOM.

HI DR. SOPHIE. CAN YOU COME AND CHECK DAISY'S NEW BABIES?

WHAT LOVELY NEWS! I'LL SEND SOME HELP RIGHT AWAY.

2 Stephanie wants to make sure that Mom and babies are healthy, so she calls Dr. Sophie for some advice.

3 Stephanie loves organizing everything, but even she finds that two baby bunnies is too much work for one person. They're so wriggly!

NOW WHERE HAS THAT OTHER BABY BUNNY GOT TO?

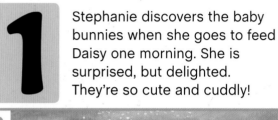

34

4 Fortunately, Dr. Sophie sends Mia and Emma to check on the bunnies. Andrea also comes to help and gets to work tidying up all the mess.

THESE BABIES ARE PERFECTLY HEALTHY. THEY'RE JUST HUNGRY!

WE'LL SOON GET THIS PLACE INTO SHAPE!

5 With three bunnies to look after, Stephanie realizes that she needs a bigger hutch. Of course, Olivia knows just what to do. She designs and builds a new hutch!

THERE'S PLENTY OF ROOM NOW AND I'VE ADDED A PLAY AREA FOR THE BABIES.

THANKS FOR YOUR HELP EVERYONE. DAISY AND I ARE VERY LUCKY!

Olivia completed the new hutch in just one day. She wanted it to be perfect for the babies.

Dream jobs

Emma, Olivia, Andrea, Stephanie, and Mia all have big plans for their futures. It won't be easy, but with hard work, talent and, of course, a little support from their friends, they know they can achieve anything.

Fashion designer

I'm going to be a fashion designer. I always know **what's hot and what's not**. I'm already working on my first collection.

Inventor

I dream of **inventing a brilliant gadget** that will make people's lives easier. If I put my mind to it, I know I can do it!

THIS IS MY BEST INVENTION YET!

Getting around
Heartlake City

Driving around town is lots of fun, especially when you have a cool set of wheels. However, Mia, Emma, and Stephanie also like to use their driving skills to help others, especially animals.

Before she sets out on a trip, Mia checks her car over with her toolkit.

Eco-car

There's plenty of space in the trunk for Mia's purse and goggles.

Mia's new car is a sleek, colorful convertible. It looks cool and, best of all, it's eco-friendly. Mia loves driving her friends and family around town in her car.

Windshield

Eco-tires

Bumper sticker

Vet ambulance

Driving the vet ambulance is a very important job. Emma not only transports sick animals, but she also gives them first-aid treatment. This little hedgehog is dehydrated, but Emma knows just how to help him. With a few sips from the feeding bottle onboard he'll be fine in no time!

Quad bike

YOU'RE SAFE NOW, YOU POOR RABBIT.

As a member of Pet Patrol, Stephanie drives around looking for lost or injured pets. Thanks to her sturdy quad bike, she can even go off road. That's Stephanie's favorite part!

Heartlake City gas station

THIS ECO-FUEL WON'T HARM THE PLANET.

Fuel pump

Caring for the planet is important to Mia so she always fills her car with eco-fuel.

Out and about

Olivia travels around town on her bicycle, while Andrea likes to take to the skies. She thinks the best way to see Heartlake City is from a hot-air balloon!

Dress to impress

Mia, Stephanie, Andrea, Emma, and Olivia have very different looks, but one thing they all agree on is that you should always wear something that makes you feel fabulous. Clothes can be practical or fancy, colorful or simple—it's up to you to choose your fashion path, and have fun with it.

A cute jacket is the perfect finishing touch for any outfit.

Fashion advice

The girls always try to make sure that their outfits fit the occasion. Whether it's a day at school or a trip to the jungle, it's important to feel comfortable.

Wear clothes in your favorite color—Mia's is green.

Cool and casual

Mia likes a relaxed, comfy look because she spends so much time being active. Paw print and butterfly motifs reflect her love of nature.

Formal fashion

Stephanie likes to dress formally at school because it makes her feel confident. Well, doesn't every straight-A student need a straight-A look?

ACCESSORIES

Emma has one golden fashion rule: accessorize, accessorize, accessorize! Co-ordinating hair clips, sunglasses, purses, or lipstick can add the perfect finishing touch to any outfit.

Lipstick

Sunglasses

Purse

Hair bow

Hair clip

A shiny black riding hat looks stylish and keeps you safe.

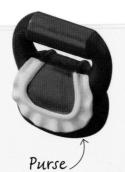

Don't get stuck in a style rut— try something new.

Andrea has a signature motif—musical notes.

Budding diva

Andrea likes to be glamorous. She always looks ready for a show-stopping performance—even if she's just going to work at the City Park Café!

Riding chic

Emma always looks picture-perfect, no matter what she's doing. For horseback riding, her trousers are pure white and her top has a subtle sparkly silver detail.

Jungle attire

Olivia usually prefers to dress casually, like Mia, but a trip to the jungle calls for something different. Olivia chooses a collared shirt teamed with a pink scarf.

Kate

Everyone at Heartlake High knows me as adventurous and energetic. I like to keep busy doing something exciting (or sometimes a little bit crazy). I like to think of myself as sporty, fun, and not afraid of anything.

> COME ON, LET'S HIT THE WATER!

Making waves

I love anything to do with the ocean—jet-skiing, surfing, snorkeling, swimming, and sailing. I spend as much time as possible at Ambersands Beach.

My stylish purple jet-ski is perfect for zooming across the bay. It's awesome!

Strawberry picking

My friends Stephanie, Mia, Andrea, Emma, and Olivia have helped me to discover new hobbies. Strawberry picking is healthy and fun—and messy!

"Life should be lived at top speed!"

My new project

I've heard about a legendary pirate called "Dark-Eyed Kate" so I've got a summer job at the lighthouse to find out more about her.

My Top 3 Activities

Watersports—you name it, I love it!

Volleyball—I play on the Heartlake High team.

Joking around—I like to tease. My friends know I'm only joking!

I'LL HAVE A DOUBLE SCOOP PLEASE— STRAWBERRY AND CHOCOLATE.

Best friends forever

I'm good friends with Stephanie. We often hang out together at her beach house, and she often comes to the lighthouse to visit me and have fun.

How to take care of animals

Animals of all kinds are welcome in Heartlake City. Whether they are furry or feathered, spiky or slimy, Mia and Emma are determined to make sure that each one is safe, healthy, and happy.

Emma carries Jojo the sick hedgehog on a special animal stretcher.

HERE'S OUR NEXT PATIENT, MIA. SHE'S SO CUTE!

Stretcher

Stethoscope

Otoscope

Mia will listen to the hedgehog's heart and check her ears for blockages.

Heartlake Vet Clinic

Thanks to Dr. Sophie's training, Mia can treat minor injuries at the new Heartlake Vet Clinic. It has an x-ray scanner and an exercise yard.

3-STEP PROGRAMME

1 Diagnosis

Mia weighs each patient and checks them over thoroughly before recommending a course of treatment.

Rehoming

If an animal doesn't have a home, Mia and Emma work with Dr. Sophie to find it a new one. Mia wishes she could keep them all herself!

Vet's hat

2 Treatment

Emma administers the medicine and makes sure she gives each patient a large dose of cuddles.

3 Home time

When the patient is fit and healthy again, Mia washes and grooms it, and sends it home as good as new.

Spring

in **Heartlake City**

Springtime is beautiful in Heartlake City. It's a time when plants bloom again after the winter and, best of all, it's when baby animals are born. Come and experience the magic of this season.

Newborn foals

Olivia has delivered **two foals**. These two cute baby horses will need lots of love and care before they are big enough to ride.

Snow the foal

Hen house

Egg-citing news

Animal expert Mia can tell that these are **no ordinary eggs**—if the hen sits on them for a little while longer they will **hatch into chicks!**

46

Waking woods

Whispering Woods

Misty the fawn loves spring. Winter in Whispering Woods is cold and quiet but spring is full of color and life.

Leaping lamb

Most **lambs** are born in spring. This poor lamb is an orphan but Stephanie is going to nurture and care for him.

Brush

Sunshine Ranch

Sunshine Ranch is busy in Spring. Mia helps to plant all the new crops. She also helps Mocca give birth to her new foal, Fame.

I THINK HE'S GOING TO BE STRONG, JUST LIKE HIS MOM.

THAT IS THE MOST ADORABLE FOAL I'VE EVER SEEN!

A day in the life of
Ms. Stevens

Being a teacher is a rewarding job. Science is my passion and I love helping students discover new things about the world around them. Over the years, I've taught thousands of students and watched them grow up into fine young adults.

Spectacles

The day begins

School starts at 8.30am but I arrive at 7.30am every day. I like to have a cup of coffee and then greet the students. Heartlake High is a very friendly place!

> GOOD MORNING STEPHANIE. SEE YOU IN SCIENCE CLASS.

> GOOD MORNING, MS. STEVENS.

Healthy apple

Cool class

I believe students like Matthew and Stephanie should discover science for themselves. My classes involve lots of exciting experiments.

SCIENCE IS FUN!

PUT THE CHEMICALS INTO THE BEAKER AND WATCH THEM TURN GREEN!

Lunchtime

The school cafeteria serves a range of healthy lunch options. I usually have a salad and some fruit, to set a good example to the students.

Lilac jacket

FINISHED! NOW I CAN GO HOME AND RELAX.

Math book

Preparation

The students finish school at 3.30pm, but I have more work to do. I have to tidy my classroom, mark homework and prepare my lessons for the next day. It's hard work, but I enjoy it.

49

Amazing animals

All animals are amazing, but Emma, Olivia, and Mia have been lucky enough to make some rare and special friends. Which one would you most like to meet?

Flame

Juliet

Juliet lives high up in the jungle treetops. Emma met the **orangutan** while working at the jungle base. Juliet thinks that Emma is the kindest person ever and loves to hang out with her new friend.

Flame the **tiger cub** loves meeting new people and exploring new places. Once she got stuck in a waterfall but Olivia rescued her. Now, Flame likes to share her adventures with Olivia.

HERE YOU GO FLAME, IT'S SNACK TIME!

Bobbi

Bobbi is the youngest **lion cub** in her pride, so she often has to stay home while the others go and hunt. While her family is away she likes to play with her friends, especially Mia.

Goldie and Java

Satin

Satin the **seal** would love to make friends with someone like Mia. They both share a passion for tricks and magic shows, but unfortunately, Satin lives in chilly Antarctica.

Mia is training Goldie the **yellow warbler** and Java the **macaw** to be lookouts. Goldie can normally be found at Olivia's treehouse and Java at the Jungle Rescue Base.

Casper

Casper the **penguin** also lives in Antarctica but he'd love to go on a trip to Heartlake City. He has a budding sense of adventure. Maybe he could adapt to live by Lake Heart?

Bamboo

Bamboo the **baby panda** was very scared and shy until he met Emma, Olivia, Mia, Andrea, and Stephanie. Now he has five new best friends and feels safe and happy at the Jungle Base.

After-school hobbies

Olivia

Surf and turf

Olivia takes surf lessons twice a week at Ambersands Beach. When she's not surfing, she heads to Sunshine Ranch and helps Mia's grandparents with their vegetable garden.

Fresh carrots

Surfboard

After a busy day learning new things at school, it's great fun to do something completely different. Olivia, Mia, Andrea, Stephanie, and Emma all have some really cool hobbies. Which one would you choose?

Stephanie

Tutus and tunes

When Stephanie wants to be sophisticated and elegant she practices ballet, but when she wants to rock out she plays her electric guitar.

Ballet studio

Mia

Drums

Tuxedo

Music and magic

Mia can often be found hitting some beats on her drum kit or preparing for the Heartlake City Magic Show. She's learning an amazing new card trick.

Hot-air balloon

Piano

Balloons and beats

Andrea practices her music every day, but she has also got an exciting new hobby—hot-air ballooning. It's a really relaxing way to travel.

Emma

Black belt

Electric guitar

Kicks and pics

Emma has been learning karate for many years, but photography is a new hobby for her. She's a natural though, and is already planning an exhibition.

Professional camera

The ♥ Heartlaker

Edited by *Stephanie*

This week:
Special jungle report, with news from Olivia and Mia!

Dramatic tiger rescue

Local hero Olivia saves the life of a poor trapped tiger cub.

Adventurous Olivia was hiking in Jungle Falls when she spotted the baby tiger struggling near a dangerous waterfall. With no thought for her own safety, the helpful Heartlaker built a dam to divert the river and pulled the frightened feline to safety. "It's just what anyone would have done," brave Olivia said afterwards.

Olivia was able to use her practical skills to save Flame.

Flame has now fully recovered, thanks to Olivia.

Matthew spotted Blu stuck in the middle of the river.

Bear trapped in bridge collapse!

Last week a hungry bear got more than he bargained for on a trip across the river.

Blu the bear just wanted to try some juicy berries, but a rotten bridge left him stranded. Fortunately, help was close by as local animal lover, Mia, was flying by in her helicopter.

She lowered her winch and lifted the frightened bear to safety. Blu was very happy to see his rescuers, Mia and Matthew!

Mia needed all her flying skills to hover in the right spot and rescue Blu.

How do friends relax?

Shopping and makeovers

When you have a busy, exciting life, it's important to take time out to relax. Emma, Mia, Olivia, Andrea, and Stephanie all have some fabulous ways to chill out. And, after some quality down-time, they will be ready for their next amazing adventure.

Emma likes to visit the mall to check out all the latest fashions.

I'M GOING TO HAVE A MANICURE, THEN A FACIAL!

Emma and Stephanie know the perfect place to chill out—the Heartlake Shopping Mall. They can shop, eat great food, or just relax in the spa. It's a great day out.

Going on vacation

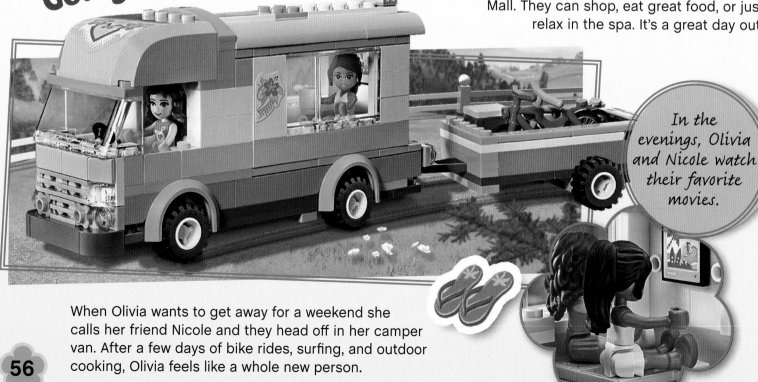

In the evenings, Olivia and Nicole watch their favorite movies.

When Olivia wants to get away for a weekend she calls her friend Nicole and they head off in her camper van. After a few days of bike rides, surfing, and outdoor cooking, Olivia feels like a whole new person.

Fun in the sun

Emma has her own private splash pool, but she lets her friends use it, too.

I THINK IT MIGHT BE TIME FOR AN ICE CREAM SOON!

Andrea heads to the City Pool when she wants to relax. It's outdoors so she can sunbathe, swim or just soak in the hot tub. Her friend Isabella often joins her poolside for a drink or an ice cream.

Lighthouse escape

Stephanie often rows over to say "hi" to this friendly seal!

Stephanie visits her friend Kate when she wants to take a break from organizing everyone. Kate has an amazing ice-cream shop next to a remote lighthouse.

Secrets of interior design

The five friends love hanging out together, but sometimes they need time out. So, each girl has created a unique space where she can relax and be by herself. Here are some top design tips for creating a personal place.

Bright colors

Be bold!

Olivia's bedroom is where she goes to switch off. She's always busy inventing something, but here she can just **chill out**. The bold, contrasting colors make her feel **relaxed** and **happy**.

Soundproof it!

Mia is full of energy, so she needs a space where she can **let loose**. She's soundproofed her bedroom so she can practice her new hobby. Playing the **drums** is a great way to relieve stress!

Mia's room is large, but she keeps it neat and tidy. Clutter is not a good look!

I CAN PLAY AS LOUD AS I LIKE WITHOUT DISTURBING ANYONE!

Plan it!

Think carefully about what you want to do in your personal space and how it should look. It will take time to create a place that's perfect for you.

I LOVE THE SOUND OF THE OCEAN. IT'S SO RELAXING.

Be with nature

Stephanie feels happiest when she's by the ocean so her special place is her beach house. It's **small** but **cozy** and has everything she needs—her surfboard, a couch, and a stereo system.

Emma's bathroom is mainly purple, with splashes of other bright colors.

Fragrance it

Emma loves to soak for hours in a fragrant, relaxing bubble bath. For Emma, how the room smells is almost as important as how it looks. Her **signature scent** is fresh and clean.

Bubble bath

Control centre

Andrea's bedroom is a hub of activity. It's where she plays, plans, and practices. Here, she **sings** in front of the mirror, updates her **blog** on her laptop, and tries out **new looks** at her dressing table.

59

Natasha

I don't think of myself as a hairdresser—I'm an artist! Hair is my canvas, and scissors, dye, and hairspray are my tools. At the Heartlake Hair Salon I like to create totally new styles and transform my clients' looks. From braids to bangs, color to curls, I'll try anything. It always looks out of this world.

Dyed pink stripe

Comb in tunic pocket

Hairbrush

Consultation

I always start by listening to my clients. They tell me what they are looking for and then I make it happen. Emma is one of my favourite clients—she's never afraid to try new looks.

WOULD YOU LIKE TO TRY A WHOLE NEW STYLE, EMMA?

I THINK YOU'D LOOK AMAZING WITH RED HAIR.

I LOVE YOUR PINK STRIPE.

Making it happen

Before cutting it, I always wash my clients' hair as it's easier to cut when it's wet. I usually give them a head massage, too: a relaxed customer is a happy customer!

The end results

When I've finished a new style, I like to show the client how it looks from every angle. Seeing a customer leave my salon feeling great about themselves gives me a warm glow. I love my job!

I LOVE IT! YOU'RE A GENIUS, NATASHA.

COME BACK AND VISIT US AGAIN SOON.

It's business

If a client loves their new style, they might buy a styling product to look after it. Emma bought a special shampoo when I dyed her hair to make the color last longer.

61

Summer

Outdoor cooking

in **Heartlake City**

Summer is Olivia, Mia, Andrea, Stephanie, and Emma's favorite season. There's no school so they can spend all their time hanging out with each other and doing their favorite things. And summer in Heartlake City is always sunny!

In the warm weather, Olivia's dad, Peter, cooks up the most amazing **barbecue feasts** for everyone. Olivia and Nicole are pretty good with a camping stove, too!

> FOOD TASTES SO MUCH BETTER COOKED OUTDOORS!

Outdoor stove

Healthy and happy

Fruit stall

Summer is a great time to be healthy. Olivia, Stephanie, and Kate love to eat lots of **fresh fruit and salads**—and an ice cream or two, of course.

Pool party

LET'S GET THIS PARTY STARTED, GIRLS!

Music player

City Pool is ideal for a summer party. It has a huge pool, a hot tub with space for both Andrea and Isabella, and a cool juice bar.

Relaxing at the beach

Ambersands Beach is a popular spot in summer. With its cool blue sea and golden sand, it's the perfect place to hang out with friends.

Sandcastle

HI THERE, YOU MUST BE SHEEN THE DOLPHIN.

How to prepare for a horse show

Entering a horse show is the perfect way for a horse and its rider to show everyone what they can do. It takes a lot of preparation, but it's great fun— even if you don't win. Come and watch Emma, Mia, Stephanie, Robert, and Katharina get ready.

Horses need lots of care and attention. They have to be fed and cleaned every day.

> I THINK MAJOR IS READY FOR THE SHOW, ROBERT.

MAJOR

Robert

> YOUR COAT IS WHITER THAN SNOW, BLAIZE.

Grooming makes a horse look and feel great. Mia talks to Blaize as she grooms him.

Katharina

Practice is very important. Katharina and Niki will need perfect technique for the show.

Basket with soap and grooming products

Jump

Emma and Robin travel to horse shows in style. They usually win the "best turned out" prize.

Showtime

Horse shows include many events, from dressage to pony racing, but the main event is always the jumping competition. Everyone wants to win it!

On the podium

Everyone performs well in the jumping competition, and Stephanie and Ruby win a top prize. Ruby is very happy to beat her stablemate, Major—he's determined to beat her next time though!

Trophy

Rosette

After the show, Ruby deserves a treat, so Stephanie gives her a tasty carrot!

RUBY

65

Theresa

I have the best summer job in the world—I'm a riding instructor at the Summer Riding Camp. I spend every day riding, grooming, and training horses, including my favorite horse, Foxie. I also teach other people how to ride, making sure they know how to handle the horses carefully and safely. Most importantly, I make sure we all have fun!

> A HORSE'S FRONT LEGS ARE CALLED THE FORELEGS.

Jodhpurs

Riding boots

The basics

I take my job very seriously. Before I allow a student on a horse, I make sure they are prepared. Here, I'm teaching Stephanie the parts of a horse, then I'll explain how to mount and dismount safely. After that, Stephanie will be ready to meet her horse.

Grooming tips

After their riding lessons, I like to show my students how to care for the horses. Here, I'm supervising Stephanie and Emma as they groom Champion.

HIS TAIL IS CLEAN AND TANGLE-FREE.

SO IS HIS MANE! GROOMING IS HARD WORK!

IT'S YOUR TURN NEXT, CHAMPION!

Camp fun

Many of the students stay at the camp for a whole week, so I also organize evening activities. Toasting marshmallows on the camp fire is always good fun.

Carriage ride

I like to mix things up. Today, I'm showing my students how much Foxie likes to give carriage rides. Tomorrow, we'll saddle up and go for a ride in the countryside.

TOASTED MARSHMALLOWS ARE DELICIOUS!

67

Top tips for keeping fit

Go for it!
Keep fit in different ways. Challenge yourself and don't be afraid to try new sports. With a bit of practice, you can do anything!

In Heartlake City, there are plenty of ways to exercise regularly to keep fit and healthy. Stephanie, Olivia, Emma, Mia, and Andrea also find it fun. Life is so much better when you're active, and there's a sport or hobby to suit everyone.

Cycling

Practical Olivia likes to combine exercise with another one of her fantastic ideas. She is going to use her bike as a **mobile ice-cream stall**. Of course, that means she'll have to make some changes to her bike. She's off to her workshop!

COME ON TEAM, LET'S WIN THIS MATCH!

Soccer

Stephanie is a talented soccer player. She loves playing in fast, action-packed matches, and nothing beats the thrill of celebrating a **winning goal** with her team mates. Stephanie plays for the Heartlake High team, along with Andrea and Emma.

Olivia can ride her bike standing up, just like a professional!

Team sports are a great way to make new friends, as well as keeping fit.

Soccer ball

68

Karate

Emma is a black belt in karate, which is the highest level. Learning karate has helped her to strengthen her body and focus her mind. She can also **chop** a wooden block in half with just her hand, which is pretty awesome.

Don't try this move until you've had a lot of training!

Skiing

Mia doesn't like to do the same sports all year round. That would be boring! In summer she hangs out at the beach and does watersports, but in winter she likes to put on her **warmest clothes** and go skiing.

Ice-skating and sledding are also fun winter sports.

Hiking

WHERE SHALL I GO TODAY? LET'S CONSULT THE MAP...

Andrea likes to keep fit while **exploring the countryside** around Heartlake City, so hiking is her favorite form of exercise. Fresh air, amazing scenery, and interesting wildlife make long walks in the great outdoors really rewarding!

Map

Andrea combines hiking with another hobby— photography.

Camera

Hazel the squirrel

Welcome to the market

Emma has turned her talents to flower arranging. She picked the flowers at Sunshine Ranch and put them in funky vases.

Every year, Heartlake City hosts a famous summer market. People travel from miles around to visit the colorful stalls, that sell everything from local crafts to mouthwatering fresh food. This year there are some extra-special stalls...

Stephanie's Bakery

WHO WANTS A FRESH STRAWBERRY ICE CREAM?

Stephanie is not only selling her famous cupcakes, she's trying out new recipes for cookies, pretzels, and sandwiches.

Good cause

The girls plan to donate their profits to Page's Pets, the pet rescue center. Mia got her dog Charlie from there and she thinks it's an amazing place.

Mia's Lemonade Stand

Lemonade pump

Lemons

Seating area

Umbrella

Popsicles

Mia had to pick lots of lemons, but it was worth it. Everyone wants a refreshing glass of her homemade lemonade.

Olivia's Ice-Cream Bike

Thanks to the sunny weather, Olivia's stall is very popular. Everyone wants to try one of her delicious ice creams. She just hopes she doesn't run out of ice-cream cones!

I DO! STRAWBERRY IS MY FAVORITE FLAVOR.

Purse

A day in the life of

Marie

My aunt opened the City Park Café many years ago. These days her homely little place is one of the most popular hangouts in Heartlake City. Every day, I work hard to make sure customers get great food and first-class service.

Lemon meringue pie

Café uniform

MY NEWEST RECIPE—CHOCOLATE AND BANANA MUFFINS!

Baking

Every day, I arrive several hours before the café opens to bake the cakes, muffins and pies that the customers love so much. My speciality is lemon meringue pie but I'm always trying out new recipes.

72

Serving

The café is always busy, but I have a hardworking team to help me out. Andrea takes the orders and I make the smoothies and serve slices of pie. Every customer should leave us with a full stomach and a happy smile.

Washing up

My least favorite chore is washing the dishes. Do you know how hard it is to clean a pan with baked-on cake mix? I just wish Olivia would invent a super-powerful dishwasher...

Home time

At the end of the day, I like to leave the café looking spotless, so I sweep up every last crumb. Then, I go home for a hot bath and a good night's sleep, before starting all over again in the morning.

73

Jungle adventure

The Jungle Rescue Base is designed to help endangered animals. The jungle is beautiful and full of amazing wildlife, but it can be a dangerous and scary place, too—as Stephanie, Andrea, and Emma discover!

1 Stephanie and Andrea use the telescope to search for animals in trouble. Emma radios via the walkie-talkie with news.

ROGER THAT, EMMA. WE'RE ON OUR WAY. OVER AND OUT!

2 Juliet the orangutan is trapped in a cave. She needs rescuing! Andrea heads for the zip wire, while Stephanie slides to the speedboat.

ACTION STATIONS EVERYONE. JULIET IS IN TROUBLE!

IF WE WORK TOGETHER, JULIET WILL SOON BE FREE.

3 In minutes, Andrea and Stephanie have reached Emma and Juliet. They need to work out a plan. Fast.

DON'T WORRY JULIET, WE'LL GET YOU OUT OF THERE.

4 Emma needs all her strength to move the rocks that are trapping Juliet. Stephanie supervises, while Andrea is on standby with the medical kit.

5 At last Juliet is free! After Andrea has checked her over, Emma settles the frightened orangutan into the special passenger seat on the rescue bike.

YOU'RE SAFE NOW, JULIET. LET'S TAKE YOU TO THE BASE.

Dr. Sophie runs the Jungle Rescue Base and she's very proud of the work the girls are doing.

IT'S SNACK TIME, JULIET. HERE'S YOUR FAVORITE— A BANANA!

6 Back at the base, the girls make Juliet feel safe and happy. When she's fully recovered they will help her return to her jungle home.

75

How to be a roving reporter

Emma loves to create, and her latest project is all about making headlines. She travels around Heartlake City in a state-of-the-art news van, seeking out the hottest stories. Emma's friend Andrew helps, too. Come and see how they make the news.

LET'S GO AND FIND SOME NEWS!

When Emma and Andrew climb into their news van they are ready for anything. It's a fully equipped **mobile TV studio!**

While Andrew plans the story, Emma makes herself **camera-ready**. She wants to look poised and perfectly professional.

THIS STORY IS HOT! IT'S JUST WHAT WE NEED.

Bingo! Andrew has a **scoop**! The world's prettiest cake is right here in Heartlake City.

And now...

...for the weather. After reading the news, Emma ends her broadcast with a weather report. It's going to be another sunny day in Heartlake City—perfect conditions for a stroll around Lake Heart.

And action!

When Emma and Andrew have checked all the facts, they are ready to share their story. Emma memorizes the script and then speaks confidently into the microphone, while Andrew films her.

The cake takes center stage. After all, this is the real story. Viewers will love it.

The news van contains vital equipment such as video cameras, lights, and microphones.

I'M HERE WITH THE WORLD'S PRETTIEST CAKE, AND IT LOOKS YUMMY, TOO!

Andrew's job is to make sure Emma and the cake are both in shot. He needs a steady hand.

77

Andrea's Alley

♪ Follow me on my daily blog

Hot-air balloon adventure

Hi there, it's time for another blog post and this one is an amazing story. And it's all true! It started when Noah and I decided to explore the caves near Clearspring Falls. The only way to get there is via hot-air balloon!

Did you know?

Hot-air balloons were actually invented long before airplanes. They are an elegant way to travel, but extremely difficult to steer!

BUT I THOUGHT YOU SAID IT WAS THIS WAY?

A little trouble

Let's just say that Noah and I weren't exactly the best of friends before this trip and things got a whole lot worse when we got a little lost. I might have had the map, but it wasn't my fault!

Clearspring Falls

After a few wrong turns, we finally made it to the top of Clearspring Falls. The stunning views made us forget our earlier mishaps and we both agreed the ride had been awesome. The caves were fantastic, too.

New friendship

Over a delicious picnic prepared by Noah, I realized that he wasn't so bad after all. He is kind, thoughtful, and fun. We thought that maybe we could be friends despite our differences, although we both agreed that it might be best if we shared the map reading for the trip back to Heartlake City!

To show that we really are friends, Noah gave me the last donut!

Great memories

It was one of the best days of my life—my first ride in a hot-air balloon, beautiful views, amazing caves, and a cool new friend. I took lots of pictures so I'll never, ever forget this adventure.

Dolphin rescue mission

Mia has been selected to join the crew of the *Dolphin Cruiser*. Along with her friends Andrew and Maya, she will search the ocean for dolphins and study their behaviour. However, it looks like some of the dolphins might need their help!

1 Mia, Maya, and Andrew take it in turns to the steer the boat. It's Andrew's turn at the moment, so Mia and Maya are relaxing with ice creams on deck.

THIS IS SUCH A FUN TRIP. I HOPE WE SEE A DOLPHIN SOON, THOUGH.

WHO'S TURN IS IT TO STEER NEXT? I NEED A BREAK!

2 Suddenly, Mia sees two dolphins, but they're in trouble! They've become separated from each other.

DOLPHINS AHOY! BUT THEY NEED OUR HELP!

Dolphins can't breathe underwater but they can swim beneath the surface for up to 15 minutes.

3 Andrew has a brilliant idea! He'll use his jet-ski to round up the dolphins and help them find each other. It's worth a try...

IT'S WORKING! THEY'VE FOUND EACH OTHER AGAIN.

4 Andrew gives the dolphins a treat to make sure they have recovered from their scary experience. After a couple of fish each, the dolphins are happy again.

DON'T WORRY, YOU'RE SAFE NOW. HAVE A FISHY SNACK!

5 The dolphins are so grateful to be rescued that they spend the whole day swimming next to the boat, so Mia and her friends can study them. Mia names them Milo and Sheen.

WHAT A DAY! DOLPHINS ARE SO INTERESTING.

6 After a busy day of rescuing and studying the dolphins, Mia and Maya are very tired. It's time for an early night!

How to create a band!

Andrea is not the only musical maestro in Heartlake City—her friends have been learning to play some cool musical instruments, too. In fact, they think they should all start a band together and put on a concert for their friends and family.

Sheet music

Electric guitar

Guitar guy

Matthew taught himself to play guitar, and he practices every day. He wants the band to play rock music, featuring plenty of cool guitar solos for him!

Drum diva

Mia loves playing the drums. it's fast, energetic, and loud! The drummer is like the heartbeat of the band—where Mia's beat leads, the other band members will follow.

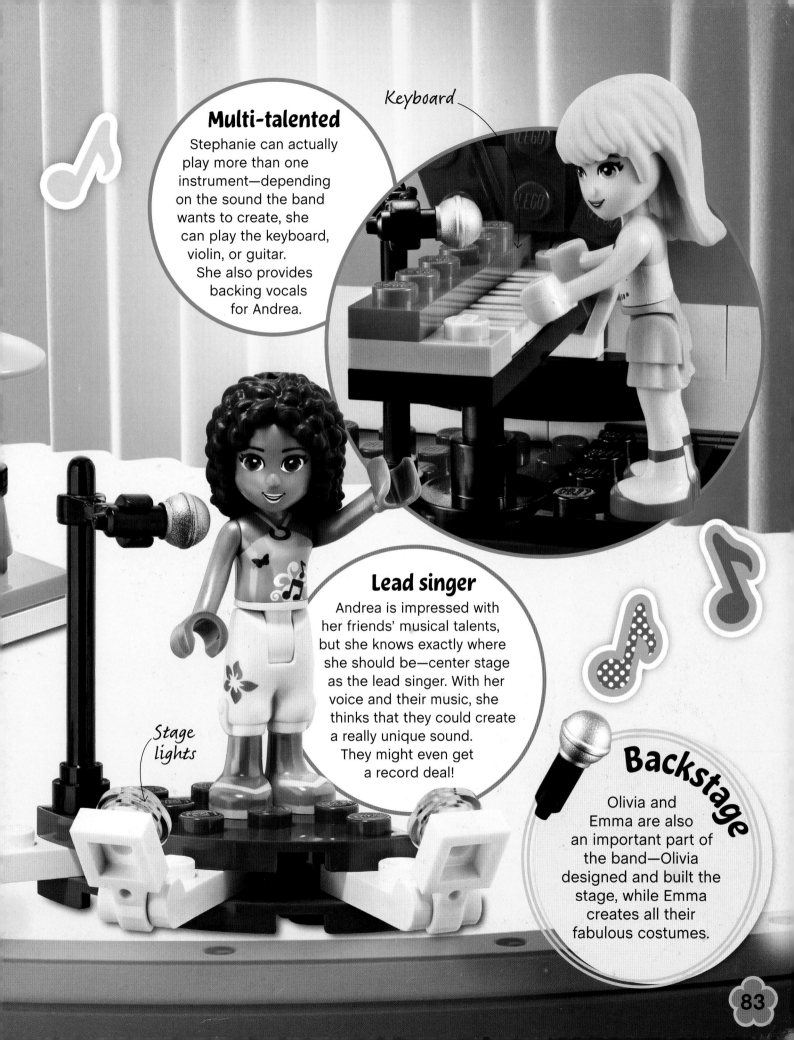

Multi-talented

Stephanie can actually play more than one instrument—depending on the sound the band wants to create, she can play the keyboard, violin, or guitar. She also provides backing vocals for Andrea.

Keyboard

Lead singer

Andrea is impressed with her friends' musical talents, but she knows exactly where she should be—center stage as the lead singer. With her voice and their music, she thinks that they could create a really unique sound. They might even get a record deal!

Stage lights

Backstage

Olivia and Emma are also an important part of the band—Olivia designed and built the stage, while Emma creates all their fabulous costumes.

What to pack for a vacation!

Going on vacation is exciting, but, whether it's sand or snow, knowing what to pack can be a real challenge. But don't worry—Emma and Mia are here to help! Follow their advice for perfect packing, wherever you're going.

Emma's top travel tip

Emma loves vacations in the sun. She takes just a few key pieces from her wardrobe, but always packs plenty of accessories so she can vary her look.

> I NEVER GO ANYWHERE WITHOUT MY HAIRDRYER!

Hairdryer

Hairbrush

Perfume

Phone

Mirror

Flippers

Sunglasses

Bucket for building sandcastles

Lipstick

Camera

Purse

Organized Mia

Before embarking on a skiing vacation, Mia always writes a list of what she needs. Warm clothes are important, but she also likes to make sure she has enough space for books.

Ski poles

Packing light

Don't take too many clothes—you won't wear them all—but do take essentials such as sunscreen, a camera, and a first-aid kit.

Skis

Binoculars

Portable radio

Hair clips

Perfume

Shampoo

WINTER VACATIONS ARE MY FAVORITE!

First-aid kit

Book about horses

Comb

Winter

in **Heartlake City**

When the snow falls on Heartlake City, it becomes a winter wonderland. For a few months of the year it is a chilly but magical place. Come and find out about the coolest things to do (and wear) in Heartlake City in winter.

Wrapping up warm

Festive cardigan

Stylish sweaters, warm boots, colored tights and chunky scarves are winter **fashion must-haves** for Christina, Mia, and Ewa.

Snow boots

Winter sports

Winter isn't a busy time for Heartlake Stables, so Theresa and the horses help deliver the mail.

When Lake Heart freezes over, it's ideal for **ice skating**. Stephanie's friend Lily is a champion ice skater. She looks so elegant!

> YOU'RE AN AMAZING ICE SKATER, LILY! CAN YOU TEACH ME?

Ice skates

Snow fun

Olivia loves building things and this year she is determined to make her biggest and best **snow sculpture** ever.

Top hat →

← *Twig arm*

Cozy chats

Mug for hot cocoa

Winter is a great time to catch up with friends over a mug of **hot chocolate**. Toasted marshmallows are perfect winter snacks, too.

← *Fir tree*

Animals in winter

Winter can be tough for some animals. Some birds fly away to warmer places, while other animals grow thicker coats and find a warm spot to **hibernate** (sleep) until spring.

Freshly fallen snow →

HI HAZEL, ARE YOU BUSY COLLECTING NUTS FOR WINTER?

87

Wish you were here!

Heartlake City is full of new places to explore and people to meet. There are also adventures to be had further afield! One of the best parts of going away is sending postcards back to friends and family, telling them about all the fun they're missing out on! Which of these exciting places would you most like to visit?

Lighthouse postcard from Kate

COME AND VISIT ME AT THE LIGHTHOUSE ANY TIME!

"A stay at the lighthouse is always busy. People love hearing all about the history of the place. I'm going to need more ice-cream supplies soon! Bye for now!"

Mountain Hut postcard from Andrea

FRESH MOUNTAIN AIR IS GREAT FOR MY VOICE!

"It's beautiful up here. Today I made a new friend—a squirrel called Hazel! I'm off to toast some marshmallows on the campfire. See you soon..."

Jungle postcard from Stephanie

DON'T FORGET YOUR SUNSCREEN IF YOU VISIT THE JUNGLE!

"The jungle is amazing! It's so full of color and life. It's pretty noisy, especially when the apes are around, but I love it here. Every day brings new challenges—just the way I like it."

89

Heartlake families

Being part of a family is amazing. From parents to siblings, grandparents to cousins, your family is always there to support, guide and love you—no matter what. Come and meet Emma and Olivia's families. Can you spot any family resemblances?

Emma's family

Emma's family is buzzing with creativity. Her mom is a successful architect, her dad is a talented interior designer, and, of course, Emma is a future fashionista.

Emma's mom, Charlotte, travels the world for her job. She's super busy but she always has time for her family.

Emma's dad, Luis, is always telling jokes—even if he is sometimes the only one who finds them funny...

MOM, DAD, I'VE HAD A GREAT IDEA FOR OUR NEW HOUSE...

Dinner time!
Emma also has two brothers—one younger and one older. In her house, mealtimes are special because they all sit down together and share news about their lives.

90

Olivia's family

Olivia's family is happy, hard-working, and helpful. Her mom is an emergency doctor and her dad is Editor-in-Chief at the NewsRoom.

Olivia's dad, Peter, cares about what's happening in the world, but he always knows what's going on in his family, too.

Olivia's mom, Anna, is full of energy. Whether it's saving lives or climbing mountains, she always gives her all.

THERE'S NEVER A DULL MOMENT IN THIS FAMILY!

Dr. Sophie is Olivia's aunt, but Olivia has to share her with the rest of Heartlake City. Everyone loves the caring vet.

Good conversation

Olivia's family, including her brother, like to talk about serious issues. They are all committed to making the world a better place, in any way they can.

Top tips for being a great friend

Emma, Olivia, Mia, Andrea, and Stephanie know how important it is to have good friends. They are always there for each other, no matter what. Here are their top tips for being a great friend.

"Be kind to each other."

"Tell your friends they look good."

No stress!

Even the best of friends sometimes have disagreements, so it is important to talk about your problems. Good friends can never stay mad at each other for long!

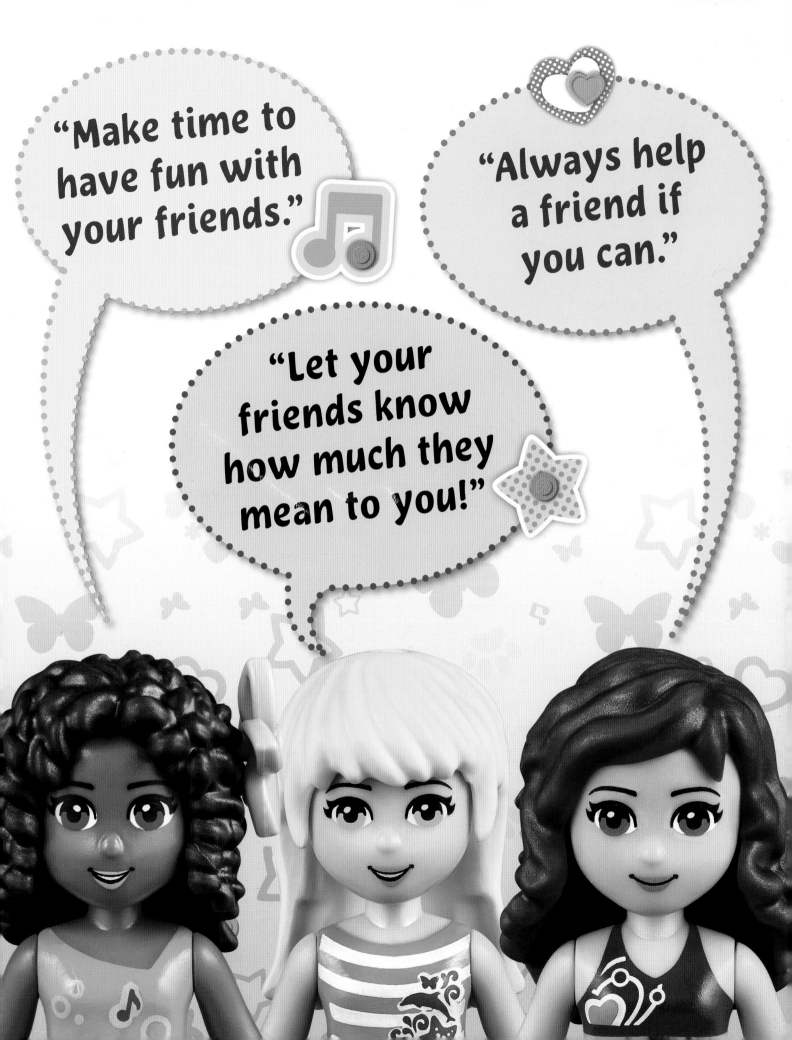

Glossary

Animal psychologist
A person whose job it is to study the behavior of animals.

Antarctica
The icy contintent around the South Pole. Animals such as penguins can be found there.

App
A special program designed for use on computers or cell phones.

Architect
A person whose job it is to design new buildings, such as houses, and make sure they are built correctly, according to the plans.

Black belt
The highest level of achievement in martial arts such as karate.

Blog
A website, such as "Andrea's Alley," through which a person records their thoughts and experiences, like an online diary.

Clinic
A vet or hospital building, where patients can be treated and receive medical help.

Dehydrated
Becoming sick due to not drinking enough fluids.

Eco-fuel
Environmentally friendly energy for vehicles such as cars, which leaves behind less harmful waste than other fuels.

Fashionista
A very fashionable person interested in creating new looks and experimenting uniquely with outfits.

Hibernate
Spending the cold winter months asleep in order to save energy. Usually referring to animals such as hedgehogs, bears, or tortoises.

Hutch
A house for keeping pets such as rabbits in.

Jodhpurs
Comfortable, stretchy pants worn specially for horseback riding.

Maestro
Someone who is very talented or an expert— usually relating to music.

Otoscope
A medical instrument for examining inside the ears of people or animals.

Pizzeria
A restaurant that specializes in making and serving pizzas.

Quad bike
A sturdy, four-wheeled motorcycle designed for traveling offroad through mud and tricky terrain.

Ranch
A farm with a large barn-like building and lots of land for animals and fruit and vegetables.

Record deal
To be given the opportunity to sing and sell songs professionally.

Jodhpurs

Stethoscope
A medical instrument for listening to people or animals' heartbeats and breathing.

Tuxedo
A formal suit, including a jacket, normally worn for formal occasions.

Vial
A strong glass jar, often used for containing chemicals or medicines.

Walkie-talkie
A type of radio used to communicate with another person.

Zip wire
A rope stretched between two high points, which can be traveled down in a hurry.

Eco-car

Index

Editor Emma Grange
Editorial Assistant Rosie Peet
Project Art Editor Lauren Adams
Designers Thelma-Jane Robb and Mark Richards
Senior Pre-Production Producer Jennifer Murray
Senior Producer Lloyd Robertson
Managing Editor Simon Hugo
Design Manager Guy Harvey
Art Director Lisa Lanzarini
Publisher Julie Ferris
Publishing Director Simon Beecroft

Dorling Kindersley would like to thank Randi Sørensen,
Paul Hansford and Robert Ekblom at the LEGO Group.

First published in the United States in 2015 by DK Publishing
345 Hudson Street, New York, New York 10014

A Penguin Random House Company

14 15 16 17 18 10 9 8 7 6 5 4 3 2 1
001–280766–Mar/15

A CIP catalogue record for this book
is available from the Library of Congress.

ISBN 978-1-4654-3549-1 (Hardcover)
ISBN 978-1-4654-3623-8 (Library Edition)

Color reproduction by Altaimage Ltd, UK
Printed and bound in China

www.LEGO.com
www.dk.com

A WORLD OF IDEAS:
SEE ALL THERE IS TO KNOW